American Hockey League

LEGENDS

By

Jim Mancuso

Mancuso Publishing

Utica, New York

For further information, contact the author at:

Mancuso Publishing
1108 Jefferson Avenue
Utica, New York 13501
(315) 733-0519
ehl1933@yahoo.com

Book & Cover Design by Jim Mancuso
Book Layout by Dave Testa
davetesta.com
dave@davetesta.com

Cover Layout by Ashley Washington

Printed by: Thompson-Shore
7300 West Joy Road
Dexter, Michigan 48130
(734) 426-3939

Note: This is not an official AHL publication. Mancuso Publishing thanks the AHL for permission to use its 75th Anniversary logo.

Jim Mancuso
American Hockey League LEGENDS

1. Author 2. Title 3. Hockey

ISBN: 978-0-9747115-3-9

SECTION BREAK PHOTOGRAPHS:

Legendary Players: (left to right): Les Binkley, Dick Mattiussi, Willie Marshall and Bill Needham.
Legendary Administrators and Head Coaches: AHL President/CEO David Andrews (center) poses with members of the 2006/07 Calder Cup champion Hamilton Bulldogs.
Legendary Graduates: (left to right): top - Bobby Bauer, George Armstrong and Pierre Pilote; middle - Billy Smith, Martin Brodeur and Brett Hull; bottom - Terry Sawchuk, Eddie Giacomin and Larry Robinson.

In Memory of AHL Legend
Jack A. Butterfield
"Chairman of the Board"
(1919-2010)

Table of Contents

PRELUDE

The American Hockey League (AHL) is celebrating its 75th Anniversary season (1936/37 to 2010/11). The AHL, known as the International-American Hockey League (IAHL) from 1936/37 to 1939/40, is the oldest minor league and is currently the longest continuously operating professional hockey loop in North America. The circuit survived the Great Depression, World War II and the minor league hockey contraction of the late 1960s and the decade of the 1970s (brought on by National Hockey League [NHL] expansion and the presence of a second major league in the World Hockey Association [WHA]). The American League served several roles in the hockey world over the years – either as an independent loop that rivaled the NHL or as a top development circuit. The AHL has had many great players within its own rank that spent their entire career (or the majority of it) in various cities around the league such as Jody Gage, Fred Glover, Willie Marshall, Gil Mayer and Fred Thurier. To its credit as a "farm" loop, there have been numerous Hockey Hall of Famers who began their pro career in the AHL such as Johnny Bower, Frank Brimsek, Eddie Giacomin, Pierre Pilote and Larry Robinson. There have also been many top-notch administrators and head coaches in the circuit. Hall of Famers Jack Butterfield, James Hendy, Frank Mathers and Eddie Shore were among the outstanding administrators (Butterfield and Mathers were elected into the prestigious institution based solely on their AHL achievements). Fred "Bun" Cook, Al MacNeil, John Paddock and John Van Boxmeer were among the excellent bench bosses.

The book features 200 outstanding figures in AHL history. The work is organized into three chapters and the celebrated individuals are arranged in alphabetical order (not ranked) – Legendary Players (150), Legendary Administrators and Head Coaches (25) and Legendary Graduates (25 players that moved up to the NHL after having played in the AHL). The legendary players were selected proportionately to the positions of a hockey team on the ice – (about) 60% are forwards, (about) 30% are defensemen and (about) 20% are goaltenders. Often times in all-time lists defensemen get overshadowed by high scoring forwards. To be considered for the legendary graduates' category one had to have played a minimum of two-thirds of one full AHL season (based on the number of games in the AHL schedule in a given season) prior to having played one-third of one full NHL season (based on the number of games in the NHL schedule in a given season) and be a member of the Hockey Hall of Fame (exception was Martin Brodeur – who will definitely be inducted).

Legend Profiles

There is a page dedicated to each legend in the book. The first line contains the **individual's proper name**. If an individual has a nickname that is more commonly used than his first name than it was put in quotation marks between his first and last name. The second line contains the individual's **predominant position** (i.e. center) **or title** (i.e. head coach). If a player had more than one regular position than each was noted. The **seasons** row(s) listed the years and the clubs that the individual was associated with while in the AHL. A <> symbol was employed to signify that the seasons played between an individual's first and last season were not consecutive (i.e. 1963/64 <> 1978/79). There is a **classic photograph** of each player in an AHL uniform (only three players are not in their AHL garb – Sid Abel, Chuck Rayner and Jack Stewart – because a photo of them in an AHL uniform could not be found). Administrators are in photos wearing their suits and head coaches are in photos wearing either their suits or their AHL team jacket. **Official AHL statistics** for players and head coaches for both the regular season and playoffs are found at the bottom of the page – statistics are through the 2009/10 season (**official NHL statistics**, also through 2009/10, are also listed in the "Legendary Graduates" chapter). The **AHL Feats** section consists of the highlights of an individual's AHL career (**NHL Feats** is also listed in the "Legendary Graduates" chapter). Below are the categories that are presented in the AHL Feats and the NHL Feats sections:

Players

1) Hockey Hall of Fame, United States Hockey Hall of Fame and AHL Hall of Fame membership
2) All-Time Regular Season Leader in points, goals, assists, hat tricks, games played and consecutive games streak
3) All-Time Regular Season Leader among defensemen in points, goals, assists and games played
4) All-Time Regular Season Leader among goaltenders in wins, shutouts, shutout sequence, games in goal and minutes played
5) All-Time Playoff Leader in points, goals, assists and games played
6) All-Time Playoff Leader among goaltenders in wins, shutouts, shutout sequence, games in goal and minutes played
7) Regular Season Career Rank for the Top 50 overall in points, goals, assists and games played
8) Regular Season Career Rank for the Top overall among defensemen in points, goals, assists and games played
9) Regular Season Career Rank for Top overall among goaltender in wins, shutouts, shutout sequence, games in goal and minutes played
10) Playoff Career Rank Top overall in points, goals, assists and games played
11) Playoff Career Rank Top overall among goaltenders in wins, shutouts, shutout sequence, games in goal and minutes played
12) Regular Season Milestone(s) for points and goals
13) Elite Achiever – player is one of a few to accomplish an amazing feat (i.e. one of two players to win three straight Les Cunningham Awards [regular season most valuable player])
14) Awards (regular season, playoff and All-Star Game) – see pages 212 & 213
15) All-Star Selections (First Team and Second Team) – 1937/38 to 2009/10
16) All-Rookie Teams – 1996/97 to 2009/10
17) Number one during the regular season in points, goals and assists (position players); wins, shutouts and goals-against average (goaltenders)
18) Top 10 during the regular season in points, goals and assists
19) Records held – regular season, playoffs and All-Star Game
20) Calder Cup winning clubs and seasons
21) Retired numbers

Head Coaches

1) Hockey Hall of Fame, United States Hockey Hall of Fame and AHL Hall of Fame
2) Elite Achiever – head coach is one of a few to accomplish an amazing feat (i.e. one of two head coaches to win back-to-back Louis A. R. Pieri Awards [outstanding coach])
3) Calder Cups won – clubs and seasons
4) Career Regular Season Rank for Top 10 in wins and in games coached
5) Louis A. R. Pieri Award (outstanding coach) – 1967/68 to the present
6) Other Awards – see pages 212 & 213
7) All-Star Selections (First Team and Second Team) – 1937/38 to 1944/45 (some seasons only one head coach was chosen, which is counted in this book as a First Team selection)
8) Regular Season titles
9) Division crowns
10) Winning regular seasons (above .500). In regard to win-loss-tie statistics for coaches, the AHL counts an overtime loss as a loss and a shootout loss as a tie.
11) Playoff qualification – percentage of seasons making the postseason

Administrators/General Managers

1) Elite Achiever – individual is one of a few to accomplish an amazing feat (i.e. one of two general managers to win four Calder Cups)
2) Thomas Ebright Award (Outstanding Contributions to the AHL) – 1997/98 to the present James C. Hendy Memorial Award (Outstanding Executive) – 1961/62 to the present Ken McKenzie Award (Outstanding Executive – Public Relations and Marketing) – 1977/78 to the present
3) Other Awards – see pages 212 & 213
4) Calder Cups won – clubs and seasons
5) Brief description of any noteworthy career highlights

Special Notes

1) All-Time Regular Season Leaders and All-Time Playoff Leaders – the first season listed after a statistical category (i.e. points) is when the player became the all-time leader and the last season listed is when his all-time record was surpassed (i.e. Fred Glover All-Time Leader in points from 1959/60 to 1970/71).
2) The only time that it is mentioned that a player was a player/head coach in the "player" chapters (Legendary Players and Legendary Graduates) was if the player won the Calder Cup or won the AHL outstanding coach award as a player/head coach.
3) The Tim Horton Trophy was presented to the top two players (a winner and a runner-up) on the roster of a Canadian-based team who accumulated the most points from the media Three Star Selections at all games during the regular season. The "winner" is noted by (W) and the "runner-up" is noted by (RU).
4) There was no official source for AHL regular season win-loss-tie statistics for goaltenders Gil Mayer and Bobby Perreault for 1958/59 (both netminders played with the Hershey Bears that season). Thus, Mayer's and Perreault's regular season career win-loss-tie totals are incomplete.
5) In order to conserve space in the AHL and NHL Feats sections for some players, administrators or head coaches, seasons were abbreviated with an apostrophe (i.e. '90 in place of 1989/90).
6) In some cases in the Legendary Players chapter if there was not any information that qualified for the AHL Feats section than the AHL Feats section was omitted.
7) Note the following abbreviations throughout the text: RS for regular season and PY for playoffs.

Dick Adolph
Defense
Seven seasons: 1938/39 to 1941/42 & 1943/44 to 1945/46, Cleveland Barons

AHL Feats: Three All-Star selections – Second Team from 1943/44 to 1945/46; Calder Cup winning clubs (three) – Cleveland in 1938/39, 1940/41 & 1944/45.

Regular Season					Playoffs				
GP	G	A	Pts.	PIM	GP	G	A	Pts.	PIM
332	26	77	103	263	58	2	12	14	58

Ralph "Red" Almas

Goaltender

Eight seasons (1946/47 to 1953/54): 1946/47 & 1947/48, Indianapolis Capitols; 1948/49 to 1952/53, St. Louis Flyers; 1953/54 Buffalo Bisons

AHL Feats: RS Career Rank – eighth in wins (218); Second All-Star Team in 1948/49.

		Regular Season								Playoffs				
GP	W	L	T	MIN	GA	Sho.	GAA	GP	W	L	MIN	GA	Sho.	GAA
450	218	192	39	27070	1590	18	3.52	9	3	6	585	32	0	3.28

Jimmy Anderson
Left Wing
16 seasons (1954/55 to 1969/70): 1954/55 to 1969/70, Springfield Indians/Kings; 1957/58, Buffalo Bisons

AHL HALL OF FAME (2009)

AHL Feats: RS Career Rank – fifth in goals (426), eighth in points (821), 11th in games played (943) and tied for 30th in assists (395); Dudley "Red" Garrett Memorial Award (outstanding rookie) in 1954/55; Two All-Star selections – Second Team in 1960/61 & 1963/64; #1 RS goals in 1960/61 & 1963/64; Top 10 RS goals in seven seasons and points in three seasons; Calder Cup winning clubs (three) – Springfield from 1959/60 to 1961/62.

		Regular Season						Playoffs		
GP	G	A	Pts.	PIM		GP	G	A	Pts.	PIM
943	426	395	821	286		37	14	3	17	4

Al Arbour
Defense
Five seasons: 1962/63 to 1966/67, Rochester Americans

HOCKEY HALL OF FAME (1996)

AHL Feats: Eddie Shore Award (outstanding defenseman) in 1964/65; Four All-Star selections – First Team from 1962/63 to 1965/66; Calder Cup winning clubs (two) – Rochester in 1964/65 & 1965/66.

	Regular Season					Playoffs				
GP	G	A	Pts.	PIM		GP	G	A	Pts.	PIM
324	15	86	101	381		39	1	6	7	42

Keith Aucoin
Center

Nine seasons (2001/02 to 2009/10): 2001/02 & 2005/06, Lowell Lock Monsters; 2002/03 & 2004/05, Providence Bruins; 2003/04, Cincinnati Mighty Ducks; 2006/07 & 2007/08, Albany River Rats; 2008/09 & 2009/10, Hershey Bears

AHL Feats: RS Career Rank – 18th in assists (441) and 31st in points (635); Les Cunningham Award (RS MVP) in 2009/10; Four All-Star selections – First Team in 2008/09 & 2009/10 and Second Team in 2005/06 & 2006/07; #1 RS assists in 2008/09 & 2009/10 and points in 2009/10 (John B. Sollenberger Trophy); Top 10 RS points and assists in five seasons and goals in one season; Calder Cup winning clubs (two) – Hershey in 2008/09 & 2009/10.

	Regular Season					Playoffs			
GP	G	A	Pts.	PIM	GP	G	A	Pts.	PIM
577	194	441	635	528	77	12	62	74	53

Pete Backor
Defense

Nine seasons: 1945/46 to 1953/54, Pittsburgh Hornets

AHL Feats: All-Time RS Leader among defensemen in assists from 1952/53 to 1955/56; Five All-Star selections – First Team in 1945/46, 1947/48 to 1949/50 & 1950/51; Skated with Calder Cup winning Pittsburgh in 1951/52.

Regular Season						Playoffs				
GP	G	A	Pts.	PIM		GP	G	A	Pts.	PIM
534	60	218	278	442		52	3	7	10	48

Jim Bartlett
Left Wing

16 seasons (1955/56 <> 1972/73): 1955/56 to 1957/58 & 1961/62 to 1965/66, Providence Reds; 1959/60, Springfield Indians; 1966/67 to 1972/73, Baltimore Clippers

AHL Feats: RS Career Rank – eighth in goals (360), 10th in games played (955), 19th in points (742) and 34th in assists (382); Top 10 RS goals in one season; Calder Cup winning clubs (two) – Providence in 1955/56 and Springfield in 1959/60; Shares RS record for fastest two consecutive goals by one player (five seconds) – set on 1/5/58 vs. Rochester @ Providence.

	Regular Season						Playoffs			
GP	G	A	Pts.	PIM		GP	G	A	Pts.	PIM
955	360	382	742	980		84	26	23	49	142

Aldege "Baz" Bastien
Goaltender
Four seasons: 1945/46 to 1948/49, Pittsburgh Hornets

AHL Feats: Elite Achiever – the only netminder to lead the circuit in RS goals-against average in three straight seasons (1946/47 to 1948/49); Harry "Hap" Holmes Memorial Award (lowest RS GAA) in 1947/48 & 1948/49 (the Holmes Award began in 1947/48); Three All-Star selections – First Team from 1946/47 to 1948/49; #1 RS shutouts from 1946/47 to 1948/49; The league instituted an award in his name (the Aldege "Baz" Bastien Memorial Award) at the start of the 1983/84 campaign that is given to the goaltender adjudged to be the best at his position.

Regular Season								Playoffs						
GP	W	L	T	MIN	GA	Sho.	GAA	GP	W	L	MIN	GA	Sho.	GAA
214	116	64	34	12840	593	19	2.77	20	10	10	1235	55	1	2.67

John Bednarski
Defense

Nine seasons (1972/73 <> 1981/82): 1972/73 & 1980/81, Rochester Americans; 1973/74 & 1974/75, Providence Reds; 1976/77 to 1978/79, New Haven Nighthawks; 1979/80, Adirondack Red Wings; 1981/82, Erie Blades

AHL Feats: Four All-Star selections – First Team in 1976/77 & 1978/79 and Second Team in 1973/74 & 1977/78; Top 10 RS assists in one season.

Regular Season						Playoffs				
GP	G	A	Pts.	PIM		GP	G	A	Pts.	PIM
576	94	285	379	1116		58	8	40	48	126

Frank Beisler
Defense

Nine seasons (1936/37 <> 1945/46): 1936/37 & 1937/38, New Haven Eagles; 1938/39 to 1941/42, Springfield Indians; 1942/43, 1943/44 & 1945/46, Buffalo Bisons

AHL Feats: Three All-Star selections – First Team in 1941/42 & 1942/43 and Second Team in 1940/41; Calder Cup winning clubs (three) – Buffalo in 1942/43, 1943/44 & 1945/46.

	Regular Season					Playoffs			
GP	G	A	Pts.	PIM	GP	G	A	Pts.	PIM
355	15	41	56	306	25	1	3	4	8

20

Gordie Bell
Goaltender

12 seasons (1942/43 <> 1955/56): 1942/43, 1949/50 & 1950/51, Buffalo Bisons; 1945/46, Providence Reds; 1946/47, Pittsburgh Hornets; 1947/48, Washington Lions; 1948/49, 1950/51, 1954/55 & 1955/56, Springfield Indians; 1951/52 to 1953/54, Syracuse Warriors

AHL Feats: Held or shared the record for shutouts in one season (nine) for over 60 seasons – established in 1942/43, shared in 2001/02 & 2002/03 and surpassed in 2003/04; RS Career Rank – 13th in wins (190) and tied for 15th in shutouts (22); First Team All-Star in 1942/43; #1 RS shutouts in 1942/43 & 1952/53 and goals-against average in 1942/43; Skated with Calder Cup winning Buffalo in 1942/43.

		Regular Season								Playoffs					
GP	W	L	T	MIN	GA	Sho.	GAA	GP	W	L	MIN	GA	Sho.	GAA
471	190	242	35	28490	1752	22	3.69	20	9	11	1217	50	1	2.47

Harvey Bennett
Goaltender

13 seasons (1946/47 to 1958/59): 1946/47, Hershey Bears; 1947/48 to 1958/59, Providence Reds

AHL Feats: All-Time RS Leader in wins in 1954/55 & 1955/56 and games in goal from 1954/55 to 1957/58; Current RS Career Rank – fourth in wins (260); Second Team All-Star in 1946/47; #1 RS wins from 1946/47 to 1948/49; Calder Cup winning clubs (three) – Hershey in 1946/47 and Providence in 1948/49 & 1955/56.

			Regular Season								Playoffs			
GP	W	L	T	MIN	GA	Sho.	GAA	GP	W	L	MIN	GA	Sho.	GAA
540	260	239	41	33260	1945	15	3.51	37	19	18	2325	111	2	2.86

Don Biggs
Center

Nine seasons (1984/85 to 1992/93): 1984/85 & 1985/86, Springfield Indians; 1985/86 & 1986/87, Nova Scotia Oilers; 1987/88 to 1989/90, Hershey Bears; 1990/91, Rochester Americans; 1991/92 & 1992/93, Binghamton Rangers

AHL Feats: In 1992/93, he garnered the highest RS point total in one season with 138 points and earned the John B. Sollenberger Trophy for being #1 RS points that year (also #1 RS goals and assists in 1992/93); RS Career Rank – tied for 21st in points (692), tied for 23rd in assists (419) and 28th in goals (273); Les Cunningham Award (RS MVP) in 1992/93; First Team All-Star in 1992/93; Top 10 RS assists in four seasons, points in three seasons and goals in one season; Skated with Calder Cup winning Hershey in 1987/88.

	Regular Season					Playoffs			
GP	G	A	Pts.	PIM	GP	G	A	Pts.	PIM
597	273	419	692	1030	70	27	52	79	110

Andy Branigan
Defense

15 seasons (1940/41 <> 1957/58): 1940/41 & 1941/42, Springfield Indians; 1945/46, Indianapolis Capitols; 1946/47 to 1953/54, Hershey Bears; 1954/55 to 1957/58, Providence Reds

AHL Feats: All-Time RS Leader in games played from 1954/55 to 1962/63; Second Team All-Star in 1955/56; Calder Cup winning clubs (two) – Hershey in 1946/47 & Providence in 1955/56.

	Regular Season						Playoffs			
GP	G	A	Pts.	PIM		GP	G	A	Pts.	PIM
859	50	171	221	995		69	4	12	16	76

Martin Brochu
Goaltender

10 seasons (1993/94 <> 2003/04): 1993/94 to 1995/96, Fredericton Canadiens; 1995/96 to 1999/2000, Portland Pirates; 2000/01, Saint John Flames; 2001/02, Manitoba Moose; 2003/04, Wilkes-Barre/Scranton Penguins

AHL Feats: RS Career Rank – 17th in wins (154); Les Cunningham Award (RS MVP) in 1999/2000; Aldege "Baz" Bastien Memorial Award (outstanding goaltender) in 1999/2000; First Team All-Star in 1999/2000; Skated with Calder Cup winning Saint John in 2000/01; All-Star Game MVP in 1999/2000.

		Regular Season								Playoffs				
GP	W	L	T	MIN	GA	Sho.	GAA	GP	W	L	MIN	GA	Sho.	GAA
363	154	137	36	19902	979	16	2.95	44	26	15	2548	103	6	2.43

Hy Buller
Defense

Eight seasons (1943/44 to 1950/51): 1943/44, Indianapolis Capitols; 1944/45 to 1947/48, Hershey Bears; 1947/48 to 1950/51, Cleveland Barons

AHL Feats: All-Time RS Leader among defensemen in points from 1950/51 to 1955/56, goals from 1950/51 to 1970/71 and assists from 1950/51 to 1952/53; Two All-Star selections – First Team in 1948/49 & 1950/51; Calder Cup winning clubs (three) – Hershey in 1946/47 and Cleveland in 1947/48 & 1950/51.

Regular Season					Playoffs				
GP	G	A	Pts.	PIM	GP	G	A	Pts.	PIM
447	79	203	282	405	63	8	22	30	47

Tom Burlington
Center

Five seasons (1942/43 to 1946/47): 1942/43 to 1945/46, Cleveland Barons; 1946/47, Providence Reds

AHL Feats: Held RS mark for most consecutive games with a point (24) for almost 40 seasons – record established in 1945/46 and broken in 1981/82; Three All-Star selections – First Team in 1943/44 & 1944/45 and Second Team in 1945/46; #1 RS points in 1943/44 and assists in 1944/45; Top 10 RS assists in four seasons and points and goals in three seasons; Skated with Calder Cup winning Cleveland in 1944/45.

Regular Season					Playoffs				
GP	G	A	Pts.	PIM	GP	G	A	Pts.	PIM
272	133	228	361	84	38	21	20	41	6

Frederic Cassivi
Goaltender

12 seasons (1995/96 <> 2007/08): 1995/96, Prince Edward Island Senators; 1996/97, Syracuse Crunch; 1997/98, Worcester IceCats; 1999/2000 to 2001/02 & 2005/06 to 2007/08, Hershey Bears; 2001/02 to 2003/04, Chicago Wolves; 2004/05, Cincinnati Mighty Ducks

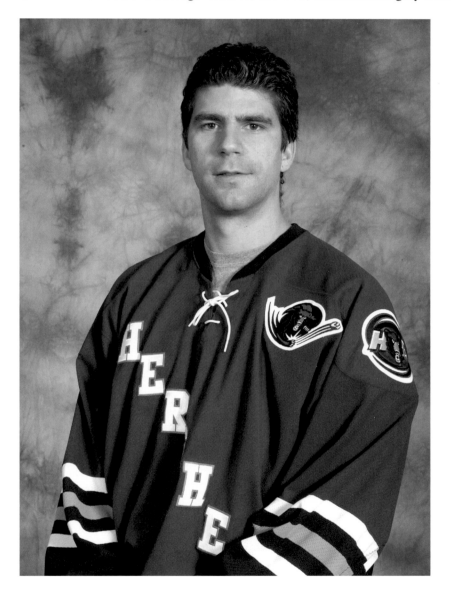

AHL Feats: Jack A. Butterfield Trophy (PY MVP) in 2005/06; RS Career Rank – fifth in wins (232) and tied for ninth in shutouts (24); #1 RS wins in 2005/06 and shutouts in 2004/05; Calder Cup winning clubs (two) – Chicago in 2001/02 and Hershey in 2005/06; Shares PY record for most wins by a goaltender in one playoff year (16) – attained in 2005/06.

			Regular Season								Playoffs			
GP	W	L	T	MIN	GA	Sho.	GAA	GP	W	L	MIN	GA	Sho.	GAA
500	232	190	47	28056	1323	24	2.83	83	46	32	4897	215	6	2.63

Ed Chadwick
Goaltender

11 seasons (1952/53 <> 1967/68): 1952/53 & 1953/54, Pittsburgh Hornets; 1954/55 & 1964/65 to 1967/68, Buffalo Bisons; 1959/60 & 1960/61, Rochester Americans; 1962/63 & 1963/64, Hershey Bears

AHL Feats: RS Career Rank – 12th in wins (196) and tied for 12th in shutouts (23); Three All-Star selections – First Team in 1959/60 and Second Team in 1960/61 & 1964/65; #1 RS shutouts in 1962/63 & 1964/65 and wins in 1959/60; Harry "Hap" Holmes Memorial Award (lowest RS GAA) in 1959/60.

		Regular Season								Playoffs				
GP	W	L	T	MIN	GA	Sho.	GAA	GP	W	L	MIN	GA	Sho.	GAA
417	196	179	28	24429	1349	23	3.31	43	21	22	2597	129	3	2.98

Don Cherry
Defense

14 seasons (1954/55 <> 1971/72): 1954/55 to 1956/57, Hershey Bears; 1957/58 to 1959/60 & 1961/62, Springfield Indians; 1963/64 to 1968/69 & 1971/72, Rochester Americans

AHL Feats: RS Career Rank – 33rd in games played (767); Calder Cup winning clubs (five) – Springfield in 1959/60 & 1961/62 and Rochester in 1964/65, 1965/66 & 1967/68.

Regular Season					Playoffs				
GP	G	A	Pts.	PIM	GP	G	A	Pts.	PIM
767	67	192	254	1066	69	7	10	17	107

Gordie Clark
Right Wing

Nine seasons (1974/75 to 1982/83): 1974/75 to 1977/78, Rochester Americans; 1978/79, Springfield Indians; 1978/79 to 1982/83, Maine Mariners

AHL Feats: RS Career Rank – tied for 30th in goals (267) and 44th in points (599); Four All-Star selections – First Team in 1979/80 & 1981/82 and Second Team in 1975/76 & 1976/77; #1 RS goals in 1979/80; Top 10 RS goals in four seasons and points and assists in three seasons; Skated with Calder Cup winning Maine in 1978/79.

	Regular Season						Playoffs			
GP	G	A	Pts.	PIM		GP	G	A	Pts.	PIM
540	267	332	599	251		94	42	48	90	33

Bruce Cline
Right Wing

13 seasons (1955/56 to 1967/68): 1955/56 to 1957/58, Providence Reds; 1958/59, Buffalo Bisons; 1959/60 to 1962/63, Springfield Indians; 1963/64 to 1967/68, Hershey Bears

AHL Feats: RS Career Rank – 12th in goals (321), 15th in points (773), tied for 15th in assists (452) and 26th in games played (823); Dudley "Red" Garrett Memorial Award (outstanding rookie) in 1955/56; Two All-Star selections – First Team in 1960/61 and Second Team in 1962/63; Top 10 RS points and goals in three seasons and assists in two seasons; Calder Cup winning clubs (four) – Providence in 1955/56 and Springfield from 1959/60 to 1961/62.

Regular Season					Playoffs				
GP	G	A	Pts.	PIM	GP	G	A	Pts.	PIM
823	321	452	773	217	89	24	34	58	31

Dave Creighton
Center

14 seasons (1948/49 <> 1968/69): 1948/49, 1950/51 & 1951/52, Hershey Bears; 1958/59 to 1960/61, Rochester Americans; 1961/62, Buffalo Bisons; 1962/63 to 1965/66, Baltimore Clippers; 1965/66 to 1968/69, Providence Reds

AHL Feats: Elite Achiever – In 1967/68, he became one of two player/head coaches (Fred Glover) to win the Les Cunningham Award (RS MVP); RS Career Rank – tied for 19th in assists (434), tied for 21st in points (692), 29th in games played (800) and 34th in goals (258); Second Team All-Star selection in 1967/68; Top 10 RS points and assists in one season.

	Regular Season					Playoffs			
GP	G	A	Pts.	PIM	GP	G	A	Pts.	PIM
800	258	434	692	390	45	15	18	33	49

Les Cunningham
Center
10 seasons: 1936/37 to 1938/39 & 1940/41 to 1946/47, Cleveland Barons/Falcons

AHL HALL OF FAME (2009)

AHL Feats: Finished AHL career after 1946/47 as the All-Time RS Leader in points and assists (both records stood until 1949/50) and as the All-Time PY Leader in points, goals, assists and games played (points and assists broke in 1948/49, goals shattered in 1949/50 and games played surpassed in 1950/51); Current RS Career Rank – tied for 47th in goals (233) and 48th in points (579) and assists (346); RS Milestone – first to score 200 goals (11/17/45 vs. Pittsburgh @ Cleveland); Five All-Star selections – First Team in 1941/42 and Second Team in 1940/41 & 1942/43 to 1944/45; #1 RS points and assists in 1940/41; Top 10 RS goals in eight seasons and points and assists in seven seasons; Calder Cup winning clubs (three) – Cleveland in 1938/39, 1940/41 & 1944/45.

	Regular Season					Playoffs			
GP	G	A	Pts.	PIM	GP	G	A	Pts.	PIM
517	233	346	579	216	58	29	33	62	13

38

Nick Damore
Goaltender

Nine seasons (1938/39 to 1946/47): 1938/39, Providence Reds; 1938/39 to 1945/46, Hershey Bears; 1946/47, Philadelphia Rockets

AHL Feats: Finished AHL career after 1946/47 as the All-Time RS Leader in wins (shattered in 1952/53), shutouts (broke in 1956/57), games in goal (surpassed in 1953/54) and longest shutout sequence (set in 1939/40 and bested in 1957/58); Current RS Career Rank – tied for fourth in shutouts (36) and ninth in wins (211); Three All-Star selections – First Team from 1943/44 to 1945/46; #1 RS wins in 1942/43 & 1943/44, shutouts in 1943/44 & 1944/45 and goals-against average in 1943/44.

		Regular Season								Playoffs				
GP	W	L	T	MIN	GA	Sho.	GAA	GP	W	L	MIN	GA	Sho.	GAA
464	211	193	61	28310	1566	36	3.32	52	27	25	3195	140	5	2.63

Craig Darby
Center/Right Wing

10 seasons (1993/94 <> 2005/06): 1993/94 & 1994/95, Fredericton Canadiens; 1995/96, Worcester IceCats; 1996/97 & 1997/98, Philadelphia Phantoms; 2001/02, Quebec Citadelles; 2002/03 & 2003/04, Albany River Rats; 2004/05, Springfield Falcons; 2005/06, Manitoba Moose

AHL Feats: RS Career Rank – 28th in assists (402) and tied for 35th in points (620); Two All-Star selections – First Team in 1997/98 and Second Team in 2002/03; #1 RS assists in 2001/02; Top 10 RS points in four seasons, assists in three seasons and goals in one season; Skated with Calder Cup winning Philadelphia in 1997/98.

	Regular Season					Playoffs			
GP	G	A	Pts.	PIM	GP	G	A	Pts.	PIM
703	218	402	620	414	50	14	24	38	8

40

Billy Dea
Center

11 seasons (1958/59 <> 1971/72): 1958/59 to 1966/67, Buffalo Bisons; 1969/70, Baltimore Clippers; 1971/72, Tidewater Wings

AHL Feats: All-Time RS Leader for most consecutive games played since 1965/66 (548 – streak of games was from 1958/59 to 1965/66); Other RS Career Rank – 41st in goals (248); Top 10 RS points in two seasons and goals and assists in one season; Skated with Calder Cup winning Buffalo in 1962/63.

	Regular Season					Playoffs			
GP	G	A	Pts.	PIM	GP	G	A	Pts.	PIM
720	248	249	497	142	48	11	16	27	6

Ab DeMarco Sr.
Center

10 seasons (1938/39 <> 1951/52): 1938/39 to 1942/43, Providence Reds; 1947/48 & 1948/49, Cleveland Barons; 1948/49, Washington Lions; 1948/49 to 1951/52, Buffalo Bisons

AHL Feats: RS Career Rank – tied for 26th in assists (409) and tied for 29th in points (638); Les Cunningham Award (RS MVP) in 1950/51; #1 RS points (Carl Liscombe Trophy) and assists in 1950/51; Top 10 RS points and assists in six seasons and goals in five seasons; Two All-Star selections – First Team in 1950/51 and Second Team in 1949/50; Calder Cup winning clubs (two) – Providence in 1939/40 and Cleveland in 1947/48.

	Regular Season					Playoffs				
GP	G	A	Pts.	PIM		GP	G	A	Pts.	PIM
544	229	409	638	225		30	5	20	25	26

Connie Dion
Goaltender

Seven seasons (1944/45 to 1950/51): 1944/45, Indianapolis Capitols; 1945/46, St. Louis Flyers; 1945/46 to 1950/51, Buffalo Bisons

AHL Feats: RS Career Rank – 14th in wins (181) and tied for 17th in shutouts (21); Harry "Hap" Holmes Memorial Award (lowest RS GAA) in 1949/50; #1 RS goals-against average also in 1945/46 (the Holmes Award began in 1947/48); Two All-Star selections – Second Team in 1945/46 & 1949/50; Skated with Calder Cup winning Buffalo in 1945/46.

			Regular Season								Playoffs			
GP	W	L	T	MIN	GA	Sho.	GAA	GP	W	L	MIN	GA	Sho.	GAA
350	181	129	40	21060	1130	21	3.22	35	15	20	2143	124	1	3.47

Kent Douglas
Defense

13 seasons (1955/56 <> 1975/76): 1955/56 & 1958/59 to 1961/62, Springfield Indians; 1963/64, 1966/67 & 1969/70, Rochester Americans; 1970/71, 1971/72 & 1973/74 to 1975/76, Baltimore Clippers

AHL Feats: Eddie Shore Award (outstanding defenseman) in 1961/62; Two All-Star selections – First Team in 1961/62 and Second Team in 1970/71; Calder Cup winning clubs (three) – Springfield from 1959/60 to 1961/62.

	Regular Season					Playoffs				
GP	G	A	Pts.	PIM		GP	G	A	Pts.	PIM
625	95	309	404	1302		74	10	28	38	153

Les Douglas
Center

11 seasons (1939/40 <> 1951/52): 1939/40 to 1942/43, 1945/46 & 1946/47, Indianapolis Capitols; 1947/48, 1948/49 & 1951/52, Buffalo Bisons; 1949/50 & 1950/51, Cleveland Barons

AHL Feats: All-Time RS Leader in assists in 1949/50 & 1950/51; Current RS Career Rank – tied for 30th in assists (395) and 34th in points (621); Les Cunningham Award (RS MVP) in 1949/50; Three All-Star selections – First Team in 1945/46 & 1949/50 and Second Team in 1946/47; #1 RS points in 1945/46 & 1949/50 (Carl Liscombe Trophy) and assists in 1949/50; Top 10 RS assists in four seasons, points in three seasons and goals in two seasons; Calder Cup winning clubs (two) – Indianapolis in 1941/42 and Cleveland in 1950/51.

Regular Season					Playoffs				
GP	G	A	Pts.	PIM	GP	G	A	Pts.	PIM
560	226	395	621	191	50	17	24	41	19

Rene Drolet
Center

15 seasons (1962/63 <> 1977/78): 1962/63 & 1964/65 to 1970/71, Quebec Aces; 1971/72 to 1973/74, Richmond Robins; 1974/75, Virginia Wings; 1975/76 to 1977/78, Rochester Americans

AHL Feats: RS Career Rank – 17th in assists (443), tied for 19th in goals (298), 20th in points (741) and games played (840); Top 10 RS points in four seasons, assists in three seasons and goals in one season.

	Regular Season					Playoffs				
GP	G	A	Pts.	PIM		GP	G	A	Pts.	PIM
840	298	443	741	300		81	31	32	63	44

Marc Dufour
Right Wing

10 seasons (1963/64 <> 1974/75): 1963/64, 1965/66 & 1970/71 to 1974/75, Baltimore Clippers; 1967/68 to 1969/70, Springfield Kings

AHL Feats: RS Career Rank – tied for 47th in goals (233), 50th in points (574) and tied for 50th in assists (341); Two All-Star selections – First Team in 1970/71 and Second Team in 1973/74; Top 10 RS goals in four seasons and points and assists in three seasons.

	Regular Season					Playoffs				
GP	G	A	Pts.	PIM		GP	G	A	Pts.	PIM
607	233	341	574	166		51	16	21	37	14

Richie Dunn
Defense

Eight seasons (1977/78 <> 1989/90): 1977/78 & 1978/79, Hershey Bears; 1984/85, Binghamton Whalers; 1985/86 to 1989/90, Rochester Americans

AHL Feats: Eddie Shore Award (outstanding defenseman) in 1984/85; Three All-Star selections – First Team in 1984/85 & 1986/87 and Second Team in 1987/88; Skated with Calder Cup winning Rochester in 1986/87.

		Regular Season						Playoffs		
GP	G	A	Pts.	PIM		GP	G	A	Pts.	PIM
428	61	199	260	296		44	6	16	22	24

Murray Eaves
Center

Nine seasons (1982/83 <> 1994/95): 1982/83 & 1983/84, Sherbrooke Jets; 1984/85 & 1985/86, Sherbrooke Canadiens; 1986/87, Nova Scotia Oilers; 1987/88 to 1989/90 & 1994/95, Adirondack Red Wings

AHL Feats: RS Career Rank – 23rd in points (680), tied for 26th in assists (409) and 29th in goals (271); Fred T. Hunt Memorial Award (sportsmanship, determination and dedication to hockey) in 1988/89 & 1989/90; Two All-Star selections – First Team in 1983/84 and Second Team in 1988/89; Top 10 RS assists in five seasons, points in four seasons and goals in three seasons; Calder Cup winning clubs (two) – Sherbrooke in 1984/85 and Adirondack in 1988/89.

	Regular Season					Playoffs			
GP	G	A	Pts.	PIM	GP	G	A	Pts.	PIM
536	271	409	680	267	52	24	40	64	57

Gerry Ehman
Left Wing/Right Wing

11 seasons (1952/53 <> 1966/67): 1952/53, St. Louis Flyers; 1956/57 & 1957/58, Springfield Indians; 1958/59, Hershey Bears; 1960/61 to 1966/67, Rochester Americans

AHL Feats: RS Career Rank – 15th in goals (311), 25th in points (676) and 39th in assists (365); Four All-Star selections – First Team in 1957/58, 1963/64 & 1965/66 and Second Team in 1960/61; #1 RS points (John B. Sollenberger Trophy) in 1963/64; Top 10 RS goals in six seasons, points in four seasons and assists in two seasons; Calder Cup winning clubs (three) – Hershey in 1958/59 and Rochester in 1964/65 & 1965/66.

Regular Season						Playoffs				
GP	G	A	Pts.	PIM		GP	G	A	Pts.	PIM
654	311	365	676	235		53	20	24	44	32

Dave Elenbaas
Goaltender
Four seasons: 1973/74 to 1976/77, Nova Scotia Voyageurs

AHL Feats: Elite Achiever – one of two netminders (Gil Mayer) to be awarded the Harry "Hap" Holmes Memorial Award (lowest team RS GAA) in four straight seasons (shared the award each year – 1973/74 to 1976/77, but was #1 RS GAA in 1975/76 & 1976/77); First Team All-Star in 1975/76; #1 RS shutouts in 1973/74, 1975/76 & 1976/77 and wins in 1975/76; Calder Cup winning clubs (two) – Nova Scotia in 1975/76 & 1976/77.

		Regular Season								Playoffs					
GP	W	L	T	MIN	GA	Sho.	GAA	GP	W	L	MIN	GA	Sho.	GAA
148	84	40	20	8660	397	14	2.75	18	10	8	1118	68	0	3.65

Dave Fenyves
Defense

12 seasons (1980/81 <> 1992/93): 1980/81 to 1984/85 & 1986/87, Rochester Americans; 1987/88 to 1992/93, Hershey Bears

AHL Feats: Eddie Shore Award (outstanding defenseman) in 1987/88 & 1988/89; Jack A. Butterfield Trophy (PY MVP) in 1986/87; Three All-Star selections – First Team in 1987/88 & 1988/89 and Second Team in 1986/87; Calder Cup winning clubs (three) – Rochester in 1982/83 & 1986/87 and Hershey in 1987/88.

Regular Season					Playoffs				
GP	G	A	Pts.	PIM	GP	G	A	Pts.	PIM
710	63	258	321	580	76	8	35	43	68

Peter Ferraro
Center/Left Wing

12 seasons (1994/95 <> 2006/07): 1994/95 to 1996/97, Binghamton Rangers; 1997/98, Hartford Wolf Pack; 1998/99 to 2000/01, Providence Bruins; 2001/02 & 2002/03, Portland Pirates; 2003/04, Springfield Falcons; 2004/05, Syracuse Crunch; 2006/07, Bridgeport Sound Tigers; 2006/07, Peoria Rivermen

AHL Feats: Jack A. Butterfield Trophy (PY MVP) in 1998/99; RS Career Rank – tied for 37th in goals (251) and 45th in points (591); First Team All-Star in 1995/96; Top 10 RS goals in two seasons and points in one season; Skated with Calder Cup winning Providence in 1998/99; Shares RS record for most power-play goals in one season (Denis Hamel, Mitch Lamoureux & Brad Smyth) – 27 in 1995/96.

	Regular Season					Playoffs			
GP	G	A	Pts.	PIM	GP	G	A	Pts.	PIM
620	251	340	591	1130	86	34	42	76	252

Dunc Fisher
Right Wing

Nine seasons (1947/48 <> 1959/60): 1947/48, New Haven Ramblers; 1952/53 to 1959/60, Hershey Bears

AHL Feats: RS Career Rank – 25th in goals (285) and tied for 35th in points (620); Five All-Star selections – First Team in 1957/58 and Second Team from 1953/54 to 1956/57; #1 RS goals in 1957/58; Top 10 RS goals in five seasons, points in four seasons and assists in two seasons; Calder Cup winning clubs (two) – Hershey in 1957/58 & 1958/59.

		Regular Season						Playoffs		
GP	G	A	Pts.	PIM		GP	G	A	Pts.	PIM
579	285	335	620	365		49	22	24	46	14

Ross Fitzpatrick
Left Wing

10 seasons (1982/83 to 1991/92): 1982/83, Maine Mariners; 1983/84, Springfield Indians; 1984/85 to 1989/90, Hershey Bears; 1990/91 & 1991/92, Binghamton Rangers

AHL Feats: RS Career Rank – tied for 17th in goals (308) and tied for 37th in points (619); Two All-Star selections – Second Team in 1985/86 & 1989/90; #1 RS assists in 1989/90; Top 10 RS points and goals in three seasons and assists in one season; Skated with Calder Cup winning Hershey in 1987/88.

	Regular Season					Playoffs			
GP	G	A	Pts.	PIM	GP	G	A	Pts.	PIM
554	308	311	619	230	79	35	24	59	52

Wade Flaherty
Goaltender

Nine seasons (1996/97 <> 2007/08): 1996/97, Kentucky Thoroughblades; 1998/99, Lowell Lock Monsters; 2001/02, Utah Grizzlies; 2002/03, San Antonio Rampage; 2003/04, Milwaukee Admirals; 2004/05 to 2006/07, Manitoba Moose; 2007/08, Rockford IceHogs

AHL Feats: Jack A. Butterfield Trophy (PY MVP) in 2003/04; RS Career Rank – tied for 17th in shutouts (21); All-Star Game co-MVP in 2005/06; Second Team All-Star in 2005/06; #1 RS shutouts in 2005/06; Skated with Calder Cup winning Milwaukee in 2003/04; Shares PY record for most wins by a goaltender in one playoff year (16) – attained in 2003/04.

		Regular Season								Playoffs					
GP	W	L	T	MIN	GA	Sho.	GAA	GP	W	L	MIN	GA	Sho.	GAA
283	138	91	26	15677	650	21	2.49	56	36	20	3444	123	3	2.14

Emile Francis
Goaltender

Seven seasons (1943/44 <> 1954/55): 1943/44, Hershey Bears; 1948/49 & 1949/50, New Haven Ramblers; 1950/51 & 1951/52, Cincinnati Mohawks; 1953/54 & 1954/55, Cleveland Barons

HOCKEY HALL OF FAME (1982)

AHL Feats: RS Career Rank – 18th in wins (146); Second Team All-Star in 1953/54; #1 RS wins and shutouts in 1953/54; Skated with Calder Cup winning Cleveland in 1953/54; The AHL initiated an award in his name (the Emile Francis Trophy) beginning with 2001/02, which is presently given to the Atlantic Division champion.

		Regular Season									Playoffs				
GP	W	L	T	MIN	GA	Sho.	GAA	GP	W	L	MIN	GA	Sho.	GAA
344	146	165	32	20780	1186	18	3.42	18	11	7	1056	58	0	3.30

Harry Frost
Right Wing

10 seasons (1938/39 <> 1949/50): 1938/39 to 1942/43 & 1945/46, Hershey Bears; 1941/42, Philadelphia Ramblers; 1946/47 to 1948/49, Springfield Indians; 1948/49, Washington Lions; 1949/50, St. Louis Flyers

AHL Feats: Three All-Star selections – First Team from 1940/41 to 1942/43; #1 RS goals in 1942/43; Top 10 RS goals in two seasons and points and assists in one season.

	Regular Season					Playoffs				
GP	G	A	Pts.	PIM		GP	G	A	Pts.	PIM
485	193	169	362	67		36	9	9	18	10

Jody Gage
Right Wing

17 seasons (1979/80 to 1995/96): 1979/80 to 1984/85, Adirondack Red Wings; 1985/86 to 1995/96, Rochester Americans

AHL HALL OF FAME (2006)

AHL Feats: All-Time PY Leader in goals from 1992/93 to 2007/08; RS Career Rank – third in points (1,048) and goals (504), fifth in games played (1,038) and sixth in assists (544); Les Cunningham Award (RS MVP) in 1987/88; Three All-Star selections – First Team in 1985/86, 1987/88 & 1990/91; #1 RS goals in 1987/88; Top 10 RS goals in six seasons, points in two seasons and assists in one season; RS record for most seasons scoring 40 or more goals (seven); Calder Cup winning clubs (three) – Adirondack in 1980/81 and Rochester in 1986/87 & 1995/96; The Americans retired his #9 (also retired for Dick Gamble).

	Regular Season						Playoffs			
GP	G	A	Pts.	PIM		GP	G	A	Pts.	PIM
1038	504	544	1048	725		115	51	59	110	94

Dick Gamble
Left Wing
14 seasons (1954/55 <> 1969/70): 1954/55 & 1957/58 to 1960/61, Buffalo Bisons; 1961/62 to 1969/70, Rochester Americans

AHL HALL OF FAME (2007)

AHL Feats: RS Career Rank – fourth in goals (468), fifth in points (892), 14th in games played (898) and 22nd in assists (424); Les Cunningham Award (RS MVP) in 1965/66; Six All-Star selections – First Team in 1960/61 & 1965/66 and Second Team in 1954/55, 1961/62, 1964/65 & 1966/67; #1 RS points (John B. Sollenberger Trophy) and goals in 1965/66; Top 10 RS goals in 10 seasons, points in four seasons and assists in two seasons; RS record for most seasons scoring 30 or more goals (11); Calder Cup winning clubs (three) – Rochester in 1964/65, 1965/66 & 1967/68; The Americans retired his #9 (also retired for Jody Gage).

Regular Season					Playoffs				
GP	G	A	Pts.	PIM	GP	G	A	Pts.	PIM
898	468	424	892	295	77	20	29	49	64

Bert Gardiner
Goaltender

Five seasons (1936/37 <> 1941/42): 1936/37 to 1939/40, Philadelphia Ramblers; 1939/40, New Haven Eagles; 1941/42, Washington Lions

AHL Feats: RS Career Rank – tied for 12th in shutouts (23); Two All-Star selections – First Team in 1938/39 and Second Team in 1939/40; #1 RS wins from 1936/37 to 1938/39, goals-against average in 1936/37 and shutouts in 1937/38.

		Regular Season								Playoffs				
GP	W	L	T	MIN	GA	Sho.	GAA	GP	W	L	MIN	GA	Sho.	GAA
238	116	97	27	14810	635	23	2.57	18	9	9	1184	43	4	2.18

Paul Gardner
Center

Seven seasons (1976/77 <> 1996/97): 1976/77, Rhode Island Reds; 1979/80, New Brunswick Hawks; 1980/81, Springfield Indians; 1983/84, Baltimore Skipjacks; 1984/85, Binghamton Whalers; 1985/86, Rochester Americans; 1996/97, Portland Pirates

AHL Feats: Elite Achiever – first and one of two (Jason Krog) to solely lead the loop in points (John B. Sollenberger Trophy), goals and assists (1984/85), first to score 60 RS goals in one season (61 in 1985/86) and one of seven (Alexandre Giroux, Phil Hergesheimer, Carl Liscombe, Brad Smyth, Guy Trottier, & Lou Trudel) to lead the circuit in RS goals in two seasons (1984/85 & 1985/86); Last to win back-to-back Les Cunningham Awards (RS MVP) – 1984/85 & 1985/86; Fred T. Hunt Memorial Award (sportsmanship, determination and dedication to hockey) in 1984/85; Two All-Star selections – First Team in 1984/85 & 1985/86; Also #1 RS points (John B. Sollenberger Trophy) in 1985/86; Top 10 RS points, goals and assists in two seasons.

Regular Season						Playoffs				
GP	G	A	Pts.	PIM		GP	G	A	Pts.	PIM
239	174	211	385	74		30	25	24	49	12

Ken Gernander
Center

14 seasons (1991/92 to 2004/05): 1991/92 to 1993/94, Moncton Hawks; 1994/95 to 1996/97, Binghamton Rangers; 1997/98 to 2004/05, Hartford Wolf Pack

AHL Feats: All-Time PY Leader in games played from 2005/06 to 2009/10; RS Career Rank – 22nd in goals (293) and tied for 32nd in points (624); Fred T. Hunt Memorial Award (sportsmanship, determination and dedication to hockey) in 1995/96 & 2003/04; Top 10 RS goals in two seasons; Skated with Calder Cup winning Hartford in 1999/2000; The Wolf Pack retired his #12.

	Regular Season					Playoffs				
GP	G	A	Pts.	PIM		GP	G	A	Pts.	PIM
973	293	331	624	341		123	26	29	55	20

Doug Gibson
Center

Seven seasons (1973/74 to 1979/80): 1973/74, Boston Braves; 1974/75 to 1976/77, Rochester Americans; 1977/78 to 1979/80, Hershey Bears

AHL Feats: Elite Achiever – first and one of three (Paul Gardner & Jason Krog) to have his hand in the league lead in RS points (John B. Sollenberger Trophy), goals (he was tied for #1) and assists (1974/75), and the only player/head coach to win the Louis A. R. Pieri Memorial Award (outstanding coach – in 1979/80); Gibson was the last player/head coach to guide a club to a Calder Cup title (Hershey in 1979/80); Les Cunningham Award (RS MVP) in 1974/75 & 1976/77; Two All-Star selections – First Team in 1974/75 & 1976/77; Top 10 RS points and assists in three seasons and goals in two seasons.

	Regular Season						Playoffs			
GP	G	A	Pts.	PIM		GP	G	A	Pts.	PIM
411	179	271	450	104		40	22	26	48	17

Jeannot Gilbert
Center

Nine seasons (1964/65 to 1972/73): 1964/65, Providence Reds; 1965/66 to 1972/73, Hershey Bears

AHL Feats: RS Career Rank – tied for 23rd in assists (419) and 28th in points (650); First Team All-Star in 1968/69; #1 RS points (John B. Sollenberger Trophy) and assists in 1968/69; Top 10 RS assists in five seasons, points in four seasons and goals in one season; Skated with Calder Cup winning Hershey in 1968/69.

	Regular Season					Playoffs			
GP	G	A	Pts.	PIM	GP	G	A	Pts.	PIM
616	231	419	650	162	46	9	25	34	18

Alexandre Giroux
Left Wing

Nine seasons (2001/02 to 2009/10): 2001/02, Grand Rapids Griffins; 2002/03 & 2003/04, Binghamton Senators; 2003/04 to 2005/06, Hartford Wolf Pack; 2006/07 to 2009/10, Hershey Bears; 2007/08, Chicago Wolves

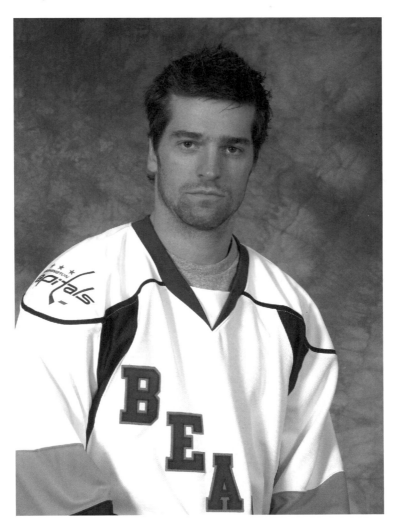

AHL Feats: RS Career Rank – tied for 17th in goals (308); Elite Achiever – one of seven to lead the loop in RS goals in two seasons (2008/09 & 2009/10 [Willie Marshall Award]); Les Cunningham Award (RS MVP) in 2008/09; Two All-Star selections – First Team in 2008/09 & 2009/10; #1 RS points (John B. Sollenberger Trophy) in 2008/09; Top 10 RS goals in five seasons, points in two seasons and assists in one season; Records for most goals in one season for RS and PY combined (75) and for most consecutive RS games with a goal (15) – both set in 2008/09; Calder Cup winning clubs (three) – Chicago in 2007/08 and Hershey in 2008/09 & 2009/10.

Regular Season					Playoffs				
GP	G	A	Pts.	PIM	GP	G	A	Pts.	PIM
636	308	264	572	774	112	50	50	100	151

Jean-Paul Gladu
Left Wing
Nine seasons (1945/46 to 1953/54): 1945/46 to 1950/51, St. Louis Flyers; 1945/46, Hershey Bears; 1951/52 to 1953/54, Providence Reds; 1951/52, Cleveland Barons

AHL Feats: RS Career Rank – 46th in goals (237); Second Team All-Star in 1947/48; Top 10 RS points and goals in two seasons.

	Regular Season					Playoffs			
GP	G	A	Pts.	PIM	GP	G	A	Pts.	PIM
522	237	246	483	230	24	11	8	19	16

Fred Glover
Right Wing

20 seasons (1948/49 to 1967/68): 1948/49 to 1951/52, Indianapolis Capitols; 1952/53, St. Louis Flyers; 1952/53 to 1967/68, Cleveland Barons

AHL HALL OF FAME (2006)

AHL Feats: All-Time RS Leader in points and assists from 1959/60 to 1970/71, goals from 1959/60 to 1971/72 and games played from 1963/64 to 1971/72 (shared games played record in 1963/64 & 1964/65); Current RS Career Rank – second in points (1,334), goals (520), assists (814) and games played (1,201); All-Time PY Leader in points from 1963/64 to 1966/67, goals from 1960/61 to 1992/93 (shared lead in 1960/61 & 1961/62 and from 1969/70 to 1992/93) and games played from 1963/64 to 2005/06; RS Milestones – first to tally 1000 points (12/12/62 @ Pittsburgh), 400 goals (3/25/62 vs. Pittsburgh @ Cleveland) and 500 goals (2/11/67 vs. Buffalo @ Cleveland); The first of two players (Willie Marshall) to appear in 20 seasons; Elite Achiever – one of two players to win the Les Cunningham Award (RS MVP) on three occasions ('60, '62 & '64); Seven All-Star selections – First Team in '51, '55, '57, '60 & '62 and Second Team in '58 & '64; Calder Cup winning clubs (five) – Indianapolis in '50 and Cleveland in '53, '54, '57 & '64 (player/head coach); The Barons retired his #9.

Regular Season					Playoffs				
GP	G	A	Pts.	PIM	GP	G	A	Pts.	PIM
1201	520	814	1334	2402	120	48	56	104	307

68

Bill Gooden
Left Wing

12 seasons (1944/45 to 1955/56): 1944/45 & 1945/46, Hershey Bears; 1945/46, New Haven Eagles; 1946/47 to 1950/51, Springfield Indians; 1951/52 to 1953/54, Syracuse Warriors; 1954/55 & 1955/56, Providence Reds

AHL Feats: RS Career Rank – tied for 37th in goals (251); Two All-Star selections – Second Team in 1944/45 & 1950/51; Top 10 RS points, goals and assists in one season; Skated with Calder Cup winning Providence in 1955/56.

		Regular Season					Playoffs			
GP	G	A	Pts.	PIM		GP	G	A	Pts.	PIM
627	251	302	553	233		23	8	7	15	20

Jack Gordon
Center

14 seasons (1947/48 to 1960/61): 1947/48 to 1949/50, New Haven Ramblers; 1950/51, Cincinnati Mohawks; 1951/52 to 1960/61, Cleveland Barons

AHL Feats: All-Time RS Leader in assists from 1957/58 to 1959/60; Current RS Career Rank – tied for 19th in assists (434) and 39th in points (615); Top 10 RS assists in five seasons, points in three seasons and goals in one season; Calder Cup winning clubs (three) – Cleveland in 1952/53, 1953/54 & 1956/57 (player/head coach).

Regular Season					Playoffs				
GP	G	A	Pts.	PIM	GP	G	A	Pts.	PIM
602	181	434	615	107	54	18	36	54	10

Mark Greig
Right Wing

10 seasons (1990/91 <> 2002/03): 1990/91 to 1993/94, Springfield Indians; 1993/94, St. John's Maple Leafs; 1994/95, Saint John Flames; 1998/99 to 2002/03, Philadelphia Phantoms

AHL Feats: RS Career Rank – 25th in assists (412), 27th in points (659) and 42nd in goals (247); First Team All-Star in 2000/01; Top 10 RS assists in four seasons, points in three seasons and goals in one season; Skated with Calder Cup winning Springfield in 1990/91.

		Regular Season						Playoffs		
GP	G	A	Pts.	PIM		GP	G	A	Pts.	PIM
606	247	412	659	848		66	17	26	43	98

Aldo Guidolin
Defense

14 seasons (1955/56 to 1968/69): 1955/56 to 1957/58 & 1965/66, Providence Reds; 1958/59, Springfield Indians; 1959/60 to 1961/62, Cleveland Barons; 1962/63 to 1964/65 & 1966/67 to 1968/69, Baltimore Clippers

AHL Feats: RS Career Rank – 16th in games played (879); Two All-Star selections – First Team in 1960/61 & 1961/62; Skated with Calder Cup winning Providence in 1955/56.

	Regular Season					Playoffs			
GP	G	A	Pts.	PIM	GP	G	A	Pts.	PIM
879	78	297	375	1662	44	7	12	19	83

Denis Hamel
Left Wing

10 seasons (1997/98 <> 2009/10): 1997/98 to 1999/2000 & 2002/03, Rochester Americans; 2003/04 to 2005/06 & 2007/08 to 2009/10, Binghamton Senators

AHL Feats: RS Career Rank – 23rd in goals (290); Yanick Dupre Memorial Award (AHL Man of the Year) in 2007/08; First Team All-Star in 2003/04; #1 RS goals (shared Willie Marshall Award) in 2005/06; Top 10 RS goals in five seasons and points in two seasons; Shares RS record for most power-play goals in one season (27) – established in 2005/06.

Regular Season					Playoffs				
GP	G	A	Pts.	PIM	GP	G	A	Pts.	PIM
710	290	265	555	802	55	14	15	29	69

Michel Harvey
Left Wing

11 seasons (1959/60 <> 1970/71): 1959/60 to 1962/63, Quebec Aces; 1963/64, 1964/65 & 1966/67 to 1970/71, Hershey Bears

AHL Feats: RS Career Rank – 40th in assists (363), 41st in points (601) and 45th in goals (238); First Team All-Star in 1968/69; Top 10 RS assists in two seasons and points and goals in one season; Skated with Calder Cup winning Hershey in 1968/69.

	Regular Season					Playoffs				
GP	G	A	Pts.	PIM		GP	G	A	Pts.	PIM
726	238	363	601	398		46	7	14	21	19

Greg Hawgood
Defense

Seven seasons (1988/89 <> 2004/05): 1988/89 & 1990/91, Maine Mariners; 1990/91 & 1991/92, Cape Breton Oilers; 2001/02 & 2002/03, Utah Grizzlies; 2003/04 & 2004/05, Chicago Wolves

AHL Feats: Eddie Shore Award (outstanding defenseman) in 1991/92; Tim Horton Trophy (Canadian-based team outstanding player – RU) in 1991/92; Two All-Star selections – First Team in 1991/92 and Second Team in 2001/02; Top 10 RS assists in one season.

	Regular Season						Playoffs			
GP	G	A	Pts.	PIM		GP	G	A	Pts.	PIM
424	79	256	335	424		24	4	9	13	68

Darren Haydar
Right Wing

Eight seasons (2002/03 to 2009/10): 2002/03 to 2005/06, Milwaukee Admirals; 2006/07 & 2007/08, Chicago Wolves; 2008/09, Grand Rapids Griffins; 2009/10, Lake Erie Monsters

AHL Feats: All-Time PY Leader in points (135) and goals (59) since 2007/08; Shared the All-Time PY Lead in assists (76) since 2009/10 (sole All-Time Leader in assists in 2008/09); RS Career Rank – 35th in assists (376) and tied for 42nd in points (600); Les Cunningham Award (RS MVP) in 2006/07; Dudley "Red" Garrett Memorial Award (outstanding rookie) in 2002/03; Two All-Star selections – First Team in 2006/07 and Second Team in 2008/09; All-Rookie Team in 2002/03; #1 RS points (John B. Sollenberger Trophy) and assists in 2006/07; Top 10 RS points in four seasons and goals and assists in three seasons; RS record for most consecutive games with a point (39) – attained in 2006/07; Calder Cup winning clubs (two) – Milwaukee in 2003/04 and Chicago in 2007/08.

Regular Season					Playoffs				
GP	G	A	Pts.	PIM	GP	G	A	Pts.	PIM
562	224	376	600	356	105	59	76	135	70

Bryan Helmer
Defense

16 seasons (1993/94 <> 2009/10): 1993/94 to 1997/98, Albany River Rats; 1998/99 & 1999/2000, Worcester IceCats; 2001/02 & 2002/03, Manitoba Moose; 2003/04, Springfield Falcons; 2004/05 & 2005/06, Grand Rapids Griffins; 2006/07 & 2007/08, San Antonio Rampage; 2008/09 & 2009/10, Hershey Bears

AHL Feats: All-Time PY Leader in games played (138) since 2009/10; RS Career Rank – seventh in games played (982); Two All-Star selections – First Team in 1997/98 and Second Team in 2005/06; Calder Cup winning clubs (three) – Albany in 1994/95 and Hershey in 2008/09 & 2009/10.

Regular Season					Playoffs				
GP	G	A	Pts.	PIM	GP	G	A	Pts.	PIM
982	120	393	513	1290	138	13	41	54	172

Gord Henry
Goaltender
11 seasons: 1944/45 to 1954/55, Hershey Bears

AHL Feats: Finished AHL career after 1954/55 as the All-Time PY Leader in shutouts (eight); All-Time RS Leader in games in goal in 1953/54 & 1954/55; Current RS Career Rank – seventh in wins (226); Second Team All-Star in 1951/52; Skated with Calder Cup winning Hershey in 1946/47.

			Regular Season								Playoffs			
GP	W	L	T	MIN	GA	Sho.	GAA	GP	W	L	MIN	GA	Sho.	GAA
510	226	230	52	30700	1839	18	3.59	49	24	24	3076	121	8	2.36

Phil Hergesheimer
Right Wing

11 seasons (1937/38 <> 1950/51): 1937/38, 1938/39, 1942/43, 1943/44 & 1945/46, Cleveland Barons; 1941/42, Hershey Bears; 1946/47 to 1948/49, Philadelphia Rockets; 1949/50 & 1950/51, Cincinnati Mohawks

AHL Feats: Finished AHL career after 1950/51 as the All-Time RS Leader in hat tricks (record surpassed in 1959/60); All-Time RS Leader in goals from 1948/49 to 1950/51; Current RS Career Rank – 24th in goals (288); Elite Achiever – one of seven to lead the circuit in RS goals in two seasons (1937/38 & 1938/39); Five All-Star selections – First Team in 1938/39, 1943/44 & 1946/47 and Second Team in 1947/48 & 1948/49; #1 RS points in 1946/47; Top 10 RS goals in six seasons, points in three seasons and assists in one season; Skated with Calder Cup winning Cleveland in 1938/39.

Regular Season					Playoffs				
GP	G	A	Pts.	PIM	GP	G	A	Pts.	PIM
548	288	265	553	107	37	22	18	40	24

Wayne Hicks
Right Wing

Nine seasons (1960/61 <> 1969/70): 1960/61 & 1961/62, Buffalo Bisons; 1963/64 to 1967/68, Quebec Aces; 1968/69 & 1969/70, Baltimore Clippers

AHL Feats: RS Career Rank – tied for 50th in assists (341); Three All-Star selections – First Team in 1966/67 and Second Team in 1964/65 & 1968/69; Top 10 RS points in four seasons, goals in three seasons and assists in one season.

Regular Season					Playoffs				
GP	G	A	Pts.	PIM	GP	G	A	Pts.	PIM
570	230	341	571	397	43	11	9	20	30

Larry Hillman
Defense

Nine seasons (1955/56 ◇ 1967/68): 1955/56, Buffalo Bisons; 1959/60, Providence Reds; 1961/62 & 1963/64 to 1967/68, Rochester Americans; 1962/63, Springfield Indians

AHL Feats: Eddie Shore Award (outstanding defenseman) in 1959/60; Two All-Star selections – First Team in 1959/60 & 1964/65; Calder Cup winning clubs (three) – Rochester in 1964/65, 1965/66 & 1967/68.

		Regular Season					Playoffs		
GP	G	A	Pts.	PIM	GP	G	A	Pts.	PIM
319	32	165	197	448	15	3	6	9	35

Bronco Horvath
Center

13 seasons (1950/51 <> 1969/70): 1950/51, Springfield Indians; 1951/52 to 1953/54, Syracuse Warriors; 1956/57 & 1962/63 to 1969/70, Rochester Americans

AHL Feats: RS Career Rank – 10th in assists (484), 17th in points (747) and 32nd in goals (263); Three All-Star selections – First Team in 1956/57 and Second Team in 1963/64 & 1964/65; Top 10 RS assists in five seasons, points in four seasons and goals in two seasons; Calder Cup winning clubs (three) – Rochester in 1964/65, 1965/66 & 1967/68.

	Regular Season					Playoffs				
GP	G	A	Pts.	PIM		GP	G	A	Pts.	PIM
666	263	484	747	416		62	15	33	48	58

Ron Ingram
Defense

12 seasons (1956/57 <> 1968/69): 1956/57 to 1962/63, 1967/68 & 1968/69, Buffalo Bisons; 1956/57, Cleveland Barons; 1964/65 to 1966/67, Baltimore Clippers

AHL Feats: Two All-Star selections – First Team in 1967/68 and Second Team in 1968/69; Calder Cup winning clubs (two) – Cleveland in 1956/57 and Buffalo in 1962/63.

	Regular Season					Playoffs			
GP	G	A	Pts.	PIM	GP	G	A	Pts.	PIM
731	66	272	338	1120	74	8	30	38	156

Ivan Irwin
Defense

Eight seasons (1949/50 <> 1959/60): 1949/50 to 1951/52, Cincinnati Mohawks; 1955/56 to 1957/58, Providence Reds; 1958/59 & 1959/60, Buffalo Bisons

AHL Feats: Three All-Star selections – First Team in 1957/58 & 1958/59 and Second Team in 1956/57; Skated with Calder Cup winning Providence in 1955/56.

Regular Season					Playoffs				
GP	G	A	Pts.	PIM	GP	G	A	Pts.	PIM
428	19	86	105	867	28	1	7	8	48

Wes Jarvis
Center

Nine seasons (1979/80 <> 1989/90): 1979/80 to 1981/82, Hershey Bears; 1984/85 & 1985/86, St. Catharines Saints; 1986/87 to 1989/90, Newmarket Saints

AHL Feats: RS Career Rank – tied for 37th in assists (366); Tim Horton Trophy (Canadian-based team outstanding player – RU) in 1985/86; Top 10 RS assists in four seasons, points in three seasons and goals in one season; Skated with Calder Cup winning Hershey in 1979/80.

	Regular Season					Playoffs				
GP	G	A	Pts.	PIM		GP	G	A	Pts.	PIM
459	205	366	571	283		33	13	29	42	22

Greg Joly
Defense

Nine seasons (1975/76 <> 1985/86): 1975/76, Richmond Robins; 1976/77, Springfield Indians; 1979/80 to 1985/86, Adirondack Red Wings

AHL Feats: Two All-Star selections – First Team in 1984/85 and Second Team in 1983/84; Calder Cup winning clubs (two) – Adirondack in 1980/81 & 1985/86.

Regular Season					Playoffs				
GP	G	A	Pts.	PIM	GP	G	A	Pts.	PIM
421	39	204	243	677	46	5	17	22	95

Walter "Jeff" Kalbfleisch
Defense

Four seasons (1936/37 to 1939/40): 1936/37, New Haven Eagles; 1936/37 & 1937/38, Providence; 1938/39 & 1939/40, Hershey Bears

AHL Feats: Three All-Star selections – First Team in 1938/39 & 1939/40 and Second Team in 1937/38; Skated with Calder Cup winning Providence in 1937/38.

	Regular Season					Playoffs			
GP	G	A	Pts.	PIM	GP	G	A	Pts.	PIM
182	11	18	29	200	16	0	1	1	6

Ralph Keller
Defense
13 seasons (1957/58 <> 1973/74): 1957/58, Providence Reds; 1962/63, Baltimore Clippers; 1963/64 to 1973/74, Hershey Bears

AHL Feats: All-Time RS Leader among defensemen in goals from 1970/71 to 1993/94; Two All-Star selections – First Team in 1968/69 and Second Team in 1972/73; Top 10 RS assists in one season; Calder Cup winning clubs (two) – Hershey in 1968/69 & 1973/74; The Bears retired his #3 (also retired for Frank Mathers).

Regular Season					Playoffs				
GP	G	A	Pts.	PIM	GP	G	A	Pts.	PIM
839	111	335	446	1330	77	11	24	35	156

Brian Kilrea
Center

10 seasons (1959/60 to 1968/69): 1959/60 to 1967/68, Springfield Indians/Kings; 1968/69, Rochester Americans

HOCKEY HALL OF FAME (2003)

AHL Feats: RS Career Rank – tied for 13th in assists (453) and tied for 32nd in points (624); #1 RS assists in 1961/62; Top 10 RS assists in five seasons and points in three seasons; Calder Cup winning clubs (three) – Springfield from 1959/60 to 1961/62.

	Regular Season					Playoffs			
GP	G	A	Pts.	PIM	GP	G	A	Pts.	PIM
622	171	453	624	242	28	4	11	15	6

Steve Kraftcheck
Defense

13 seasons (1949/50 <> 1963/64): 1949/50 & 1953/54 to 1957/58, Cleveland Barons; 1950/51, Indianapolis Capitols; 1958/59 to 1961/62, Rochester Americans; 1962/63 & 1963/64, Providence Reds

AHL HALL OF FAME (2008)

AHL Feats: All-Time RS Leader among defensemen in assists (386) since 1961/62 and in points from 1961/62 to 2005/06; Other RS Career Rank – 33rd overall in assists (386) and tied for 21st overall in games played (839); Elite Achiever – one of three players (Pete Leswick & Jim Morrison) to be selected an all-star in six straight seasons (First Team from 1956/57 to 1959/60 and Second Team in 1955/56 & 1960/61); Eddie Shore Award (outstanding defenseman) in 1958/59; Calder Cup winning clubs (two) – Cleveland in 1953/54 & 1956/57.

Regular Season					Playoffs				
GP	G	A	Pts.	PIM	GP	G	A	Pts.	PIM
839	67	386	453	524	74	6	31	37	66

Jason Krog
Center

Eight seasons (1999/2000 <> 2009/10): 1999/2000 & 2000/01, Lowell Lock Monsters; 1999/2000, Providence Bruins; 2000/01, Springfield Falcons; 2001/02, Bridgeport Sound Tigers; 2002/03, Cincinnati Mighty Ducks; 2006/07, 2007/08 & 2009/10, Chicago Wolves; 2008/09, Manitoba Moose

AHL Feats: Elite Achiever – In 2007/08, he became the only player to win the RS (Les Cunningham Award) and the PY most valuable player (Jack A. Butterfield Award) awards in the same season and became the second player to solely lead the league in RS points (John B. Sollenberger Trophy), goals (Willie Marshall Award) and assists; Shared All-Time PY Lead in assists (76) since 2009/10; RS Career Rank – tied for 45th in assists (352); Two All-Star selections – First Team in 2007/08 and Second Team in 2008/09; Top 10 RS points and assists in four seasons and goals in one season; Skated with Calder Cup winning Chicago in 2007/08; Shares PY record for most assists in one playoff year (26) – set in 2007/08.

		Regular Season						Playoffs		
GP	G	A	Pts.	PIM		GP	G	A	Pts.	PIM
455	171	352	523	169		101	42	76	118	33

Arnie Kullman
Center

12 seasons: 1948/49 to 1959/60, Hershey Bears

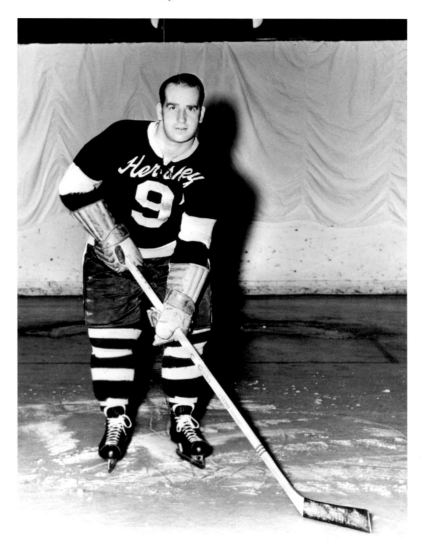

AHL Feats: RS Career Rank – 35th in games played (753), tied for 35th in goals (253), tied for 37th in points (619) and tied for 37th in assists (366); Top 10 RS points in two seasons and goals and assists in one season; Calder Cup winning clubs (two) – Hershey in 1957/58 & 1958/59; Shares All-Star Game record for career assists (six) and career games played (six); The Bears retired his #9 (also retired for Tim Tookey).

	Regular Season					Playoffs				
GP	G	A	Pts.	PIM		GP	G	A	Pts.	PIM
753	253	366	619	602		58	16	24	40	84

Jason LaBarbera
Goaltender

Seven seasons (2000/01 to 2006/07): 2000/01 to 2004/05, Hartford Wolf Pack; 2005/06 & 2006/07, Manchester Monarchs

AHL Feats: RS Career Rank – seventh in shutouts (28); Les Cunningham Award (RS MVP) in 2003/04; Aldege "Baz" Bastien Memorial Award (outstanding goaltender) in 2003/04 & 2006/07; Harry "Hap" Holmes Memorial Award (lowest team RS GAA) in 2004/05 (shared) & 2006/07; Two All-Star selections – First Team in 2003/04 & 2006/07; #1 RS wins in 2003/04 & 2006/07 and shutouts in 2003/04 & 2006/07; Record for shutouts in one season (13) – established in 2003/04.

			Regular Season								Playoffs			
GP	W	L	T	MIN	GA	Sho.	GAA	GP	W	L	MIN	GA	Sho.	GAA
247	131	75	20	13798	495	28	2.15	35	18	17	2222	83	4	2.24

Jean-Francois Labbe
Goaltender

10 seasons (1993/94 to 2002/03): 1993/94 & 1994/95, Prince Edward Island Senators; 1995/96, Cornwall Aces; 1996/97, Hershey Bears; 1997/98, Hamilton Bulldogs; 1998/99 to 2000/01, Hartford Wolf Pack; 2000/01 to 2002/03, Syracuse Crunch

AHL Feats: RS Career Rank – eighth in shutouts (27) and 11th in wins (202); Les Cunningham Award (RS MVP) in 1996/97; Aldege "Baz" Bastien Memorial Award (outstanding goaltender) in 1996/97; Harry "Hap" Holmes Memorial Award (lowest team RS GAA) in 1996/97 (#1 in GAA that season) & 1999/2000 (shared); Two All-Star selections – First Team in 1996/97 and Second Team in 2001/02; #1 RS shutouts in 1996/97 & 2001/02 and wins in 1996/97; Just the fifth goaltender (and one of 10 overall) to score a RS goal (2/5/00 at Quebec); Calder Cup winning clubs (two) – Hershey in 1996/97 and Hartford in 1999/2000.

| | | Regular Season | | | | | | | | Playoffs | | | | |
GP	W	L	T	MIN	GA	Sho.	GAA	GP	W	L	MIN	GA	Sho.	GAA
420	202	151	52	24204	1116	27	2.77	82	46	35	4934	207	7	2.52

94

Gordon Labossiere
Center

Seven seasons (1963/64 <> 1971/72): 1963/64 & 1964/65, Baltimore Clippers; 1965/66 & 1966/67, Quebec Aces; 1968/69 & 1969/70, Springfield Kings; 1971/72, Cleveland Barons

AHL Feats: Two All-Star selections – First Team in 1966/67 and Second Team in 1969/70; #1 RS points (John B. Sollenberger Trophy) in 1966/67; Top 10 RS points in five seasons, assists in four seasons and goals in three seasons.

	Regular Season					Playoffs				
GP	G	A	Pts.	PIM		GP	G	A	Pts.	PIM
406	209	291	500	505		36	9	12	21	63

Mitch Lamoureux
Center

14 seasons (1982/83 <> 1998/99): 1982/83 to 1985/86, Baltimore Skipjacks; 1986/87 to 1988/89, 1993/94, 1994/95, 1997/98 & 1998/99, Hershey Bears; 1989/90, Maine Mariners; 1995/96 & 1996/97, Providence Bruins

AHL Feats: RS Career Rank – seventh in goals (364), ninth in points (816), tied for 15th in assists (452) and 28th in games played (802); Dudley "Red" Garrett Memorial Award (outstanding rookie) in 1982/83; Fred T. Hunt Memorial Award (sportsmanship, determination and dedication to hockey) in 1998/99; Second Team All-Star in 1982/83; #1 RS goals in 1982/83; Top 10 RS points and goals in four seasons and assists in two seasons; Skated with Calder Cup winning Hershey in 1987/88; Shares RS record for most power-play goals in one season (27) – attained in 1993/94; The Bears retired his #16 (also retired for Willie Marshall).

	Regular Season					Playoffs			
GP	G	A	Pts.	PIM	GP	G	A	Pts.	PIM
802	364	452	816	1139	70	20	31	51	128

John LeBlanc
Right Wing

Eight seasons (1986/87 <> 1994/95): 1986/87 & 1987/88, Fredericton Express; 1988/89 & 1989/90, Cape Breton Oilers; 1991/92 to 1993/94, Moncton Hawks; 1994/95, Springfield Falcons

AHL Feats: RS Career Rank – tied for 30th in goals (267); Tim Horton Trophy (Canadian-based team outstanding player – W) in 1992/93; #1 RS goals in 1989/90; Top 10 RS goals in four seasons and points in one season.

Regular Season						Playoffs				
GP	G	A	Pts.	PIM		GP	G	A	Pts.	PIM
429	267	211	478	254		56	18	16	34	58

Michael Leighton
Goaltender

Seven seasons (2001/02 to 2007/08): 2001/02 to 2004/05, Norfolk Admirals; 2005/06, Rochester Americans; 2006/07, Portland Pirates; 2006/07, Philadelphia Phantoms; 2007/08, Albany River Rats

AHL Feats: RS Career Rank – sixth in shutouts (29); Aldege "Baz" Bastien Memorial Award (outstanding goaltender) in 2007/08; First Team All-Star in 2007/08; All-Rookie Team in 2001/02; #1 RS shutouts in 2007/08; PY record for lowest goals-against average in one playoff year (1.18) – set in 2007/08.

		Regular Season								Playoffs					
GP	W	L	T	MIN	GA	Sho.	GAA	GP	W	L	MIN	GA	Sho.	GAA
266	128	105	25	15696	602	29	2.30	19	9	8	1200	27	5	1.35

Art Lesieur
Defense

Five seasons (1936/37 to 1940/41): 1936/37 to 1939/40, Providence Reds; 1940/41, Pittsburgh Hornets

AHL Feats: Two All-Star selections – Second Team in 1937/38 & 1938/39; Calder Cup winning clubs (two) – Providence in 1937/38 & 1939/40.

Regular Season					Playoffs				
GP	G	A	Pts.	PIM	GP	G	A	Pts.	PIM
238	22	31	53	191	23	0	1	1	18

Pete Leswick
Left Wing/Right Wing
Eight seasons (1936/37 <> 1950/51): 1936/37, New Haven Eagles; 1944/45 & 1945/46, Indianapolis Capitols; 1946/47 to 1949/50, Cleveland Barons; 1950/51, Buffalo Bisons

AHL Feats: Elite Achiever – one of three players to be chosen to six all-star teams in a row (First Team in 1945/46, 1947/48 to 1949/50 and Second Team in 1944/45 & 1946/47); Top 10 RS points in five seasons, goals in four seasons and assists in three seasons; Skated with Calder Cup winning Cleveland in 1947/48.

Regular Season						Playoffs				
GP	G	A	Pts.	PIM		GP	G	A	Pts.	PIM
400	216	265	481	93		32	7	10	17	2

Carl Liscombe
Left Wing

Eight seasons (1936/37 <> 1949/50): 1936/37 & 1937/38, Pittsburgh Hornets; 1939/40 & 1940/41, Indianapolis Capitols; 1946/47, St. Louis Flyers; 1946/47 to 1949/50, Providence Reds

AHL Feats: RS Milestone – first player to tally 100 points in one season (118 points in 1947/48); Elite Achiever – one of seven to lead the loop in RS goals in two seasons (1947/48 & 1948/49); Les Cunningham Award (RS MVP) in 1947/48 & 1948/49; Jack Fox Memorial Trophy (sportsmanship) in 1948/49; Two All-Star selections – First Team in 1947/48 and Second Team in 1948/49; #1 RS points (Wally Kilrea Award) in 1947/48; Top 10 RS goals in three seasons, points in two seasons and assists in one season; Skated with Calder Cup winning Providence in 1948/49.

Regular Season					Playoffs				
GP	G	A	Pts.	PIM	GP	G	A	Pts.	PIM
354	176	206	382	100	32	6	5	11	8

Neil Little
Goaltender

11 seasons (1993/94 <> 2004/05): 1993/94 to 1995/96, Hershey Bears; 1996/97, 1997/98 & 1999/2000 to 2004/05, Philadelphia Phantoms

AHL Feats: RS Career Rank – 10th in wins (203); #1 RS wins in 1997/98; Calder Cup winning clubs (two) – Philadelphia in 1997/98 & 2004/05.

			Regular Season								Playoffs			
GP	W	L	T	MIN	GA	Sho.	GAA	GP	W	L	MIN	GA	Sho.	GAA
419	203	146	41	23370	1080	18	2.77	53	31	21	3125	123	5	2.36

Norm Locking
Left Wing

Eight seasons (1936/37 to 1943/44): 1936/37 to 1939/40, Syracuse Stars; 1936/37, Buffalo Bisons; 1940/41 to 1943/44, Cleveland Barons

AHL Feats: RS Milestone – first to score 100 goals (2/4/41 vs. Pittsburgh @ Cleveland); Three All-Star selections – First Team in 1939/40 & 1940/41 and Second Team in 1942/43; #1 RS points and goals in 1939/40; Top 10 RS points and goals in three seasons and assists in two seasons; Calder Cup winning clubs (two) – Syracuse in 1936/37 and Cleveland in 1940/41.

		Regular Season					Playoffs			
GP	G	A	Pts.	PIM		GP	G	A	Pts.	PIM
384	157	196	353	152		44	7	20	27	10

Mark Lofthouse
Right Wing

12 seasons (1977/78 to 1988/89): 1977/78 to 1980/81, 1987/88 & 1988/89, Hershey Bears; 1981/82 & 1982/83, Adirondack Red Wings; 1983/84 to 1986/87, New Haven Nighthawks

AHL Feats: RS Career Rank – 27th in goals (281) and 40th in points (606); #1 RS points (John B. Sollenberger Trophy) and goals in 1980/81; Two All-Star selections – First Team in 1980/81 and Second Team in 1983/84; Top 10 RS points and assists in two seasons and goals in one season; Calder Cup winning clubs (two) – Hershey in 1979/80 & 1987/88.

Regular Season					Playoffs				
GP	G	A	Pts.	PIM	GP	G	A	Pts.	PIM
575	281	325	606	551	50	19	24	43	56

Bill MacKenzie
Defense

Five seasons (1939/40 ◇ 1944/45): 1939/40, Providence Reds; 1940/41 to 1942/43 & 1944/45, Cleveland Barons

AHL Feats: Four All-Star selections – First Team in 1940/41 & 1941/42 and Second Team in 1939/40 & 1942/43; Calder Cup winning clubs (three) – Providence in 1939/40 and Cleveland in 1940/41 & 1944/45.

	Regular Season					Playoffs			
GP	G	A	Pts.	PIM	GP	G	A	Pts.	PIM
188	24	39	63	108	25	2	5	7	11

Ed MacQueen
Defense
16 seasons (1954/55 <> 1970/71): 1954/55 to 1956/57 & 1958/59, Cleveland Barons; 1958/59 to 1965/66, Providence Reds; 1965/66 to 1970/71, Baltimore Clippers

AHL Feats: Skated with Calder Cup winning Cleveland in 1956/57.

Regular Season					Playoffs				
GP	G	A	Pts.	PIM	GP	G	A	Pts.	PIM
850	123	263	386	891	38	4	9	13	48

Ralph MacSweyn
Defense

Seven seasons (1967/68 <> 1975/76): 1967/68 to 1970/71, Quebec Aces; 1971/72 & 1974/75, Richmond Robins; 1975/76, Baltimore Clippers

AHL Feats: Two All-Star selections – First Team in 1970/71 and Second Team in 1971/72.

		Regular Season					Playoffs			
GP	G	A	Pts.	PIM		GP	G	A	Pts.	PIM
406	12	95	107	293		28	0	14	14	54

Steve Maltais
Left Wing

Eight seasons (1989/90 <> 2004/05): 1989/90 & 1990/91, Baltimore Skipjacks; 1991/92, Halifax Citadels; 1993/94, Adirondack Red Wings; 2001/02 to 2004/05, Chicago Wolves

AHL Feats: Second Team All-Star in 2003/04; #1 RS points (John B. Sollenberger Trophy) and assists in 2002/03; Top 10 RS points, goals and assists in one season; Skated with Calder Cup winning Chicago in 2001/02; The Wolves retired his #11.

Regular Season					Playoffs				
GP	G	A	Pts.	PIM	GP	G	A	Pts.	PIM
525	213	295	508	504	92	37	51	88	86

Norm Maracle
Goaltender

Seven seasons (1994/95 <> 2002/03): 1994/95 to 1998/99, Adirondack Red Wings; 2001/02 & 2002/03, Chicago Wolves

AHL Feats: RS Career Rank – tied for 20th in wins (143); Two All-Star selections – Second Team in 1996/97 & 1997/98; #1 RS wins in 1996/97; Skated with Calder Cup winning Chicago in 2001/02.

		Regular Season								Playoffs				
GP	W	L	T	MIN	GA	Sho.	GAA	GP	W	L	MIN	GA	Sho.	GAA
333	143	130	35	18570	910	20	2.94	18	4	12	918	45	2	2.94

Willie Marshall
Center

20 seasons (1952/53 to 1971/72): 1952/53 to 1955/56, Pittsburgh Hornets; 1956/57 to 1962/63, Hershey Bears; 1958/59 & 1971/72, Rochester Americans; 1963/64 to 1965/66, Providence Reds; 1966/67 to 1970/71, Baltimore Clippers

AHL HALL OF FAME (2006)

AHL Feats: All-Time RS Leader in points (1375 – since 1970/71), goals (523 – since 1971/72), assists (852 – since 1970/71), hat tricks (25 – since 1959/60) and games played (1205 – since 1971/72); Shared record for most seasons played (20) since 1971/72; All-Time PY Leader in points in 1962/63, 1963/64 & 1966/67 to 2007/08, assists from 1962/63 to 2008/09 and shared the lead for goals from 1969/70 to 1992/93; Three All-Star selections – First Team in 1955/56 & 1957/58 and Second Team in 1961/62; #1 RS points (John B. Sollenberger Trophy) and assists in 1957/58; Top 10 RS assists in 11 seasons, points in 10 seasons and goals in nine seasons; Calder Cup winning clubs (three) – Pittsburgh in 1954/55 and Hershey in 1957/58 & 1958/59; The Bears retired his #16 (also retired for Mitch Lamoureux).

Regular Season					Playoffs				
GP	G	A	Pts.	PIM	GP	G	A	Pts.	PIM
1205	523	852	1375	520	112	48	71	119	43

Frank Mathers
Defense
14 seasons (1948/49 to 1961/62): 1948/49 to 1955/56, Pittsburgh Hornets; 1956/57 to 1961/62, Hershey Bears

HOCKEY HALL OF FAME (1992) AND AHL HALL OF FAME (2006)

AHL Feats: All-Time RS Leader among defensemen in points and assists from 1955/56 to 1961/62; Current RS Career Rank – 30th in games played (799); Six All-Star selections – First Team from 1951/52 to 1955/56 and Second Team in 1957/58; Top 10 RS assists in three seasons; Calder Cup winning clubs (four) – Pittsburgh in 1951/52 & 1954/55 and as player/coach with Hershey in 1957/58 & 1958/59; In 1996, the AHL inaugurated the Frank S. Mathers Trophy, which is presently awarded to the Eastern Conference regular season champion; The Bears retired his #3 (also retired for Ralph Keller).

	Regular Season					Playoffs			
GP	G	A	Pts.	PIM	GP	G	A	Pts.	PIM
799	67	340	407	636	86	9	35	44	64

Gil Mayer
Goaltender

14 seasons (1949/50 to 1962/63): 1949/50 to 1955/56, Pittsburgh Hornets; 1956/57 to 1958/59, Hershey Bears; 1959/60 & 1960/61, Cleveland Barons; 1961/62 & 1962/63, Providence Reds

AHL HALL OF FAME (2007)

AHL Feats: All-Time RS Leader in games in goal from 1960/61 to 1970/71 and the All-Time PY Leader in longest shutout sequence from 1950/51 to 1961/62; Current RS Career Rank – second in shutouts (41) and third in wins* (346); Elite Achiever – Harry "Hap" Holmes Memorial Award (lowest RS GAA) more times than any other goaltender (five – 1950/51 & 1952/53 to 1955/56) and one of two netminders to earn the award in four straight seasons; Five All-Star selections – First Team in 1950/51, 1953/54 & 1954/55 and Second Team in 1952/53 & 1955/56; #1 RS shutouts in 1950/51, 1951/52, 1954/55 & 1955/56 and wins in 1951/52; Calder Cup winning clubs (four) – Pittsburgh in 1951/52 & 1954/55 and Hershey in 1957/58 & 1958/59.

			Regular Season*								Playoffs			
GP	W	L	T	MIN	GA	Sho.	GAA	GP	W	L	MIN	GA	Sho.	GAA
680	346	258	57	41008	1974	41	2.89	63	37	26	4169	158	6	2.27

* - Does not include W-L-T totals from 1958/59.

Bob McCord
Defense

12 seasons (1954/55 <> 1966/67): 1954/55 to 1962/63, Springfield Indians; 1964/65, Hershey Bears; 1965/66 & 1966/67, Pittsburgh Hornets

AHL Feats: Eddie Shore Award (outstanding defenseman) in 1960/61 & 1966/67; Five All-Star selections – First Team in 1960/61 & 1966/67 and Second Team in 1959/60, 1961/62 & 1962/63; Calder Cup winning clubs (four) – Springfield from 1959/60 to 1961/62 and Pittsburgh in 1966/67.

	Regular Season					Playoffs			
GP	G	A	Pts.	PIM	GP	G	A	Pts.	PIM
635	81	252	333	551	59	4	22	26	89

Glenn Merkosky
Left Wing

10 seasons (1980/81 <> 1990/91): 1980/81 & 1981/82, Binghamton Whalers; 1983/84 & 1984/85, Maine Mariners; 1985/86 to 1990/91, Adirondack Red Wings

AHL Feats: RS Career Rank – 11th in goals (325), 24th in points (678), 41st in games played (737) and tied for 43rd in assists (353); Fred T. Hunt Memorial Award (sportsmanship, determination and dedication to hockey) in 1986/87 & 1990/91; Two All-Star selections – First Team in 1986/87 and Second Team in 1984/85; #1 RS goals in 1986/87; Top 10 RS goals in two seasons and points in one season; Calder Cup winning clubs (three) – Maine in 1983/84 and Adirondack in 1985/86 & 1988/89.

		Regular Season					Playoffs		
GP	G	A	Pts.	PIM	GP	G	A	Pts.	PIM
737	325	353	678	420	107	39	51	90	73

Alfie Moore
Goaltender

Six seasons (1936/37 to 1941/42): 1936/37 & 1940/41, New Haven Eagles; 1937/38, Pittsburgh Hornets; 1938/39 & 1939/40, Hershey Bears; 1939/40, Indianapolis Capitols; 1940/41, Springfield Indians; 1940/41, Cleveland Barons; 1941/42, Philadelphia Ramblers; 1941/42, Buffalo Bisons

AHL Feats: Finished AHL career at the end of 1941/42 after playing with eight different clubs – a record that stood until it was broken during 2001/02; RS Career Rank – tied for ninth in shutouts (24); #1 RS goals-against average and shutouts in 1938/39; Second Team All-Star in 1938/39; Skated with Calder Cup winning Cleveland in 1940/41.

		Regular Season									Playoffs				
GP	W	L	T	MIN	GA	Sho.	GAA	GP	W	L	MIN	GA	Sho.	GAA
200	89	83	28	12400	527	24	2.55	16	7	9	1012	44	0	2.61

Jim Morrison
Defense

12 seasons (1951/52 <> 1972/73): 1951/52, Hershey Bears; 1951/52, Pittsburgh Hornets; 1960/61 to 1967/68, Quebec Aces; 1968/69, 1971/72 & 1972/73, Baltimore Clippers

AHL Feats: Elite Achiever – voted to more all-star teams than any other player (eight times – First Team in 1965/66 and Second Team in 1961/62, 1963/64, 1964/65, 1966/67 to 1968/69 & 1971/72) and one of three players to be selected to the all-star team six seasons in a row; Eddie Shore Award (outstanding defenseman) in 1965/66; Top 10 RS assists in one season; Skated with Calder Cup winning Pittsburgh in 1951/52.

	Regular Season					Playoffs			
GP	G	A	Pts.	PIM	GP	G	A	Pts.	PIM
721	85	341	426	556	61	12	27	39	66

Cleland "Keke" Mortson
Center

13 seasons (1953/54 <> 1973/74): 1953/54, Cleveland Barons; 1960/61 to 1962/63, Hershey Bears; 1963/64 to 1966/67, Quebec Aces; 1968/69 & 1969/70, Baltimore Clippers; 1970/71, Rochester Americans; 1971/72, Cincinnati Swords; 1973/74, Jacksonville Barons

AHL Feats: RS Career Rank – 29th in assists (400) and tied for 42nd in points (600); Second Team All-Star in 1965/66; #1 RS assists in 1965/66; Top 10 RS assists in five seasons and points in three seasons; Skated with Calder Cup winning Cleveland in 1953/54.

	Regular Season					Playoffs			
GP	G	A	Pts.	PIM	GP	G	A	Pts.	PIM
576	200	400	600	758	61	19	34	53	139

Curtis Murphy
Defense

Five seasons (2001/02 <> 2006/07): 2001/02, 2002/03, 2005/06 & 2006/07, Houston Aeros; 2003/04, Milwaukee Admirals

AHL Feats: Eddie Shore Award (outstanding defenseman) in 2002/03 & 2003/04; Three All-Star selections – First Team in 2002/03, 2003/04 & 2005/06; Top 10 RS assists in one season; Calder Cup winning clubs (two) – Houston in 2002/03 and Milwaukee in 2003/04.

Regular Season					Playoffs				
GP	G	A	Pts.	PIM	GP	G	A	Pts.	PIM
394	76	190	266	317	67	8	23	31	48

Terry Murray
Defense

Seven seasons (1970/71 <> 1980/81): 1970/71, Providence Reds; 1971/72, Boston Braves; 1971/72, Baltimore Clippers; 1975/76, Richmond Robins; 1977/78, Philadelphia Firebirds; 1977/78 to 1980/81, Maine Mariners

AHL Feats: Eddie Shore Award (outstanding defenseman) in 1977/78 & 1978/79; Three All-Star selections – First Team in 1975/76, 1977/78 & 1978/79; Top 10 RS assists in one season; Calder Cup winning clubs (two) – Maine in 1977/78 & 1978/79.

	Regular Season					Playoffs			
GP	G	A	Pts.	PIM	GP	G	A	Pts.	PIM
363	37	159	196	261	50	5	19	24	51

Bill Needham
Defense
15 seasons: 1956/57 to 1970/71, Cleveland Barons

AHL Feats: Finished AHL career after 1970/71 having played more RS games than any other defenseman (981); Other RS Career Rank – eighth overall in games played; All-Time RS Leader in most consecutive games played from 1961/62 to 1965/66; Eddie Shore Award (outstanding defenseman) in 1967/68; First Team All-Star in 1967/68; Calder Cup winning clubs (two) – Cleveland in 1956/57 & 1963/64.

	Regular Season					Playoffs			
GP	G	A	Pts.	PIM	GP	G	A	Pts.	PIM
981	62	246	308	859	76	0	13	13	77

Mike Nykoluk
Center

16 seasons (1956/57 to 1971/72): 1956/57 & 1957/58, Rochester Americans; 1958/59 to 1971/72, Hershey Bears

AHL HALL OF FAME (2007)

AHL Feats: RS Career Rank – third in assists (686), fourth in games played (1,069) and sixth in points (881); Les Cunningham Award (RS MVP) in 1966/67; Two All-Star selections – First Team in 1967/68 and Second Team in 1966/67; #1 RS assists in 1966/67 & 1967/68; Top 10 RS assists in seven seasons and points in two seasons; Calder Cup winning clubs (two) – Hershey in 1958/59 & 1968/69; The Bears retired his #8.

		Regular Season					Playoffs			
GP	G	A	Pts.	PIM		GP	G	A	Pts.	PIM
1069	195	686	881	455		112	16	62	78	49

Eddie Olson
Left Wing

Nine seasons (1946/47 to 1954/55): 1946/47 to 1950/51, St. Louis Flyers; 1950/51 to 1954/55, Cleveland Barons

UNITED STATES HOCKEY HALL OF FAME (1977)

AHL Feats: RS Career Rank – 41st in assists (359) and 49th in points (575); Les Cunningham Award (RS MVP) in 1952/53; Two All-Star selections – First Team in 1952/53 & 1954/55; #1 RS points in 1952/53 (Carl Liscombe Trophy) & 1954/55 (John B. Sollenberger Trophy) and goals in 1954/55; Top 10 RS points, goals and assists in three seasons; Calder Cup winning clubs (three) – Cleveland in 1950/51, 1952/53 & 1953/54.

Regular Season					Playoffs				
GP	G	A	Pts.	PIM	GP	G	A	Pts.	PIM
593	216	359	575	383	49	11	33	44	57

Marcel Paille
Goaltender

15 seasons (1956/57 <> 1973/74): 1956/57, Cleveland Barons; 1957/58 & 1965/66 to 1971/72, Providence Reds; 1958/59, Buffalo Bisons; 1959/60 to 1961/62, Springfield Indians; 1962/63, Baltimore Clippers; 1973/74, Richmond Robins

AHL HALL OF FAME (2010)

AHL Feats: All-Time RS Leader in games in goal (765) and minutes played (45,300) since 1970/71; Other RS Career Rank – second in wins (349), tied for fourth in shutouts (36) and 34th overall in games played (765); Finished AHL career after 1973/74 as the All-Time PY Leader in wins (49), games in goal (87), minutes played (5,368) and longest shutout sequence (207:27 – established in 1961/62); Harry "Hap" Holmes Memorial Award (lowest RS GAA) in 1960/61 & 1961/62; Five All-Star selections – First Team in 1958/59, 1960/61 & 1961/62 and Second Team in 1956/57 & 1959/60; #1 RS wins in 1956/57, 1958/59 & 1960/61 and shutouts in 1956/57 & 1960/61; Calder Cup winning clubs (four) – Cleveland in 1956/57 and Springfield from 1959/60 to 1961/62.

Regular Season								Playoffs						
GP	W	L	T	MIN	GA	Sho.	GAA	GP	W	L	MIN	GA	Sho.	GAA
765	349	339	68	45300	2545	36	3.37	87	49	38	5368	238	5	2.66

Dennis Patterson
Defense

13 seasons (1970/71 to 1982/83): 1970/71 & 1971/72, Cleveland Barons; 1972/73, Cleveland/Jacksonville Barons; 1973/74, New Haven Nighthawks; 1974/75, Baltimore Clippers; 1975/76, Springfield Indians; 1976/77, Rhode Island Reds; 1977/78 to 1982/83, Maine Mariners

AHL Feats: Three All-Star selections – Second Team from 1978/79 to 1980/81; Calder Cup winning clubs – Maine in 1977/78 & 1978/79.

	Regular Season					Playoffs			
GP	G	A	Pts.	PIM	GP	G	A	Pts.	PIM
686	29	219	248	681	77	4	22	26	133

Bob Perreault
Goaltender

13 seasons (1951/52 ◇ 1968/69): 1951/52 & 1952/53, Providence Reds; 1956/57, 1962/63 & 1965/66 to 1968/69, Rochester Americans; 1957/58 to 1961/62, Hershey Bears

AHL Feats: RS Career Rank – third in shutouts (37) and sixth in wins* (229); Harry "Hap" Holmes Memorial Award (lowest RS GAA) in 1958/59 & 1967/68; Four All-Star selections – Second Team in 1957/58, 1958/59, 1961/62 & 1967/68; #1 RS shutouts in 1958/59, 1959/60, 1966/67 & 1967/68 and wins in 1961/62 & 1967/68; Calder Cup winning clubs (four) – Hershey in 1957/58 & 1958/59 and Rochester in 1965/66 & 1967/68.

Regular Season*								Playoffs						
GP	W	L	T	MIN	GA	Sho.	GAA	GP	W	L	MIN	GA	Sho.	GAA
503	229	176	36	29104	1475	37	3.04	83	46	36	5044	235	8	2.8

* - Does not include W-L-T totals from 1958/59.

Michel Picard
Left Wing

Nine seasons (1989/90 <> 2003/04): 1989/90, Binghamton Whalers; 1990/91 & 1991/92, Springfield Indians; 1993/94, Portland Pirates; 1994/95 & 1995/96, Prince Edward Island Senators; 2000/01, Philadelphia Phantoms; 2002/03 & 2003/04, Grand Rapids Griffins

AHL Feats: RS Career Rank – 26th in goals (283), tied for 29th in points (638) and 42nd in assists (355); Four All-Star selections – First Team in 1990/91 & 1994/95 and Second Team in 1993/94 & 2002/03; #1 RS goals in 1990/91; Top 10 RS points and goals in three seasons and assists in two seasons; Calder Cup winning clubs (two) – Springfield in 1990/91 and Portland in 1993/94; Shares RS record for most unassisted goals in one game (three) – attained in 1994/95.

Regular Season					Playoffs				
GP	G	A	Pts.	PIM	GP	G	A	Pts.	PIM
582	283	355	638	530	88	37	34	71	96

Harry Pidhirny
Center

17 seasons (1948/49 <> 1965/66): 1948/49, Philadelphia Rockets; 1949/50, 1950/51 & 1954/55 to 1960/61, Springfield Indians; 1951/52 to 1953/54, Syracuse Warriors; 1962/63, Providence Reds; 1963/64 to 1965/66, Baltimore Clippers

AHL Feats: All-Time RS Leader in games played from 1962/63 to 1964/65 (shared record in 1963/64 & 1964/65); Current RS Career Rank – third in games played (1,071), sixth in goals (376), seventh in points (829) and tied for 13th in assists (453); Second Team All-Star in 1958/59; #1 RS assists in 1958/59; Top 10 RS goals in five seasons, points in two seasons and assists in one season; Calder Cup winning clubs (two) – Springfield in 1959/60 & 1960/61; Shares RS record for most goals in one game (six) – set on 11/21/53 vs. Buffalo @ Syracuse.

	Regular Season					Playoffs			
GP	G	A	Pts.	PIM	GP	G	A	Pts.	PIM
1071	376	453	829	162	51	14	17	31	4

Noel Price
Defense

13 seasons (1956/57 <> 1975/76): 1956/57 & 1957/58, Rochester Americans; 1959/60 to 1961/62, 1969/70 & 1971/72, Springfield Indians/Kings; 1962/63 to 1964/65, Baltimore Clippers; 1965/66 & 1966/67, Quebec Aces; 1971/72 & 1975/76, Nova Scotia Voyageurs

AHL HALL OF FAME (2008)

AHL Feats: Elite Achiever – only blueliner to win the Eddie Shore Award (outstanding defenseman) on three occasions (1969/70, 1971/72 & 1975/76); RS Career Rank – 37th in games played (751); Four All-Star selections – First Team in 1969/70, 1971/72 & 1975/76 and Second Team in 1965/66; Calder Cup winning clubs (five) – Springfield from 1959/60 to 1961/62 and Nova Scotia in 1971/72 & 1975/76.

Regular Season					Playoffs				
GP	G	A	Pts.	PIM	GP	G	A	Pts.	PIM
751	59	319	378	975	78	8	31	39	118

Marc Reaume
Defense
11 seasons (1954/55 <> 1970/71): 1954/55 & 1955/56, Pittsburgh Hornets; 1960/61 to 1963/64, Hershey Bears; 1965/66 to 1968/69 & 1970/71, Rochester Americans

AHL Feats: Eddie Shore Award (outstanding defenseman) in 1962/63; Two All-Star selections – First Team in 1962/63 and Second Team in 1967/68; Calder Cup winning clubs (three) – Pittsburgh in 1954/55 and Rochester in 1965/66 & 1967/68.

		Regular Season						Playoffs		
GP	G	A	Pts.	PIM		GP	G	A	Pts.	PIM
405	30	117	147	296		51	6	11	17	60

Ed Reigle
Defense

Eight seasons (1944/45 <> 1954/55): 1944/45 & 1945/46, Indianapolis Capitols; 1949/50 & 1951/52 to 1954/55, Cleveland Barons; 1950/51, Hershey Bears

AHL Feats: Two All-Star selections – Second Team in 1951/52 & 1952/53; Calder Cup winning clubs (two) – Cleveland in 1952/53 & 1953/54.

Regular Season						Playoffs				
GP	G	A	Pts.	PIM		GP	G	A	Pts.	PIM
390	42	185	227	520		33	2	15	17	40

Wayne Rivers
Right Wing

10 seasons (1961/62 <> 1971/72): 1961/62 to 1966/67, Hershey Bears; 1968/69 & 1969/70, Buffalo Bisons; 1970/71, Baltimore Clippers; 1971/72, Springfield Kings

AHL Feats: RS Career Rank – tied for 37th in goals (251); Three All-Star selections – First Team in 1971/72 and Second Team in 1966/67 & 1970/71; #1 RS goals in 1971/72; Top 10 RS goals in three seasons and points in two seasons; Skated with Calder Cup winning Buffalo in 1969/70.

	Regular Season					Playoffs			
GP	G	A	Pts.	PIM	GP	G	A	Pts.	PIM
490	251	253	504	432	51	10	21	31	35

Moe Roberts
Goaltender

Six seasons (1936/37 to 1941/42): 1936/37 to 1941/42, Cleveland Barons/Falcons; 1941/42, Pittsburgh Hornets

UNITED STATES HOCKEY HALL OF FAME (2005)

AHL Feats: RS Career Rank – tied for 15th in shutouts (22); Two All-Star selections – First Team in 1939/40 and Second Team in 1937/38; #1 RS goals-against average and shutouts in 1939/40; Calder Cup winning clubs (two) – Cleveland in 1938/39 & 1940/41.

		Regular Season								Playoffs				
GP	W	L	T	MIN	GA	Sho.	GAA	GP	W	L	MIN	GA	Sho.	GAA
273	122	105	43	16922	720	22	2.55	15	9	5	1057	31	4	1.76

Fred Robertson
Defense
10 seasons (1936/37 to 1945/46): 1936/37 to 1943/44, Cleveland Barons/Falcons; 1943/44 & 1944/45, Pittsburgh Hornets; 1944/45 & 1945/46, Hershey Bears; 1945/46, St. Louis Flyers

AHL Feats: Three All-Star selections – First Team in 1939/40 and Second Team in 1940/41 & 1941/42; Calder Cup winning clubs (two) – Cleveland in 1938/39 & 1940/41.

	Regular Season					Playoffs			
GP	G	A	Pts.	PIM	GP	G	A	Pts.	PIM
462	31	73	104	335	40	1	7	8	50

Geordie Robertson
Right Wing

10 seasons (1979/80 to 1988/89): 1979/80 to 1984/85 & 1988/89, Rochester Americans; 1985/86 to 1987/88, Adirondack Red Wings

AHL Feats: RS Career Rank – 44th in goals (239), 47th in points (582) and 49th in assists (343); Top 10 RS assists in four seasons, points in three seasons and goals in two seasons; Calder Cup winning clubs (two) – Rochester in 1982/83 and Adirondack in 1985/86.

	Regular Season					Playoffs			
GP	G	A	Pts.	PIM	GP	G	A	Pts.	PIM
531	239	343	582	636	73	24	31	55	123

134

Darren Rumble
Defense

14 seasons (1989/90 <> 2004/05): 1989/90 to 1991/92, 1995/96 & 2003/04, Hershey Bears; 1992/93, New Haven Senators; 1993/94 & 1994/95, Prince Edward Island Senators; 1996/97, Philadelphia Phantoms; 1999/2000 to 2001/02, Worcester IceCats; 2002/03 & 2004/05, Springfield Falcons

AHL Feats: Eddie Shore Award (outstanding defenseman) in 1996/97; Two All-Star selections – First Team in 1996/97 and Second Team in 1994/95; Top 10 RS assists in one season.

Regular Season					Playoffs				
GP	G	A	Pts.	PIM	GP	G	A	Pts.	PIM
723	91	365	456	713	52	0	24	24	51

Duane Rupp
Defense

11 seasons (1961/62 <> 1976/77): 1961/62, Springfield Indians; 1962/63 & 1963/64, Baltimore Clippers; 1963/64 to 1966/67, 1975/76 & 1976/77, Rochester Americans; 1968/69, Cleveland Barons; 1971/72 & 1973/74, Hershey Bears

AHL Feats: Three All-Star selections – Second Team in 1965/66, 1966/67 & 1973/74; Calder Cup winning clubs (four) – Springfield in 1961/62, Rochester in 1964/65 & 1965/66 and Hershey in 1973/74.

		Regular Season						Playoffs		
GP	G	A	Pts.	PIM		GP	G	A	Pts.	PIM
537	48	206	254	473		56	2	28	30	80

Sam St. Laurent
Goaltender

13 seasons (1979/80 to 1991/92): 1979/80 to 1985/86, Maine Mariners; 1986/87 to 1989/90, Adirondack Red Wings; 1990/91 & 1991/92, Binghamton Rangers

AHL Feats: RS Career Rank – 16th in wins (164); Aldege "Baz" Bastien Memorial Award (outstanding goaltender) in 1985/86; Harry "Hap" Holmes Memorial Award (lowest team RS GAA) in 1985/86 (shared); Jack A. Butterfield Trophy (PY MVP) in 1988/89; Two All-Star selections – Second Team in 1984/85 & 1985/86; #1 RS shutouts in 1984/85; Calder Cup winning clubs (two) – Maine in 1983/84 and Adirondack in 1988/89.

		Regular Season								Playoffs				
GP	W	L	T	MIN	GA	Sho.	GAA	GP	W	L	MIN	GA	Sho.	GAA
359	164	139	32	20453	1199	9	3.52	66	35	29	3896	223	3	3.43

Reggie Savage
Center

10 seasons (1990/91 <> 2003/04): 1990/91 to 1992/93, Baltimore Skipjacks; 1993/94 & 1994/95, Cornwall Aces; 1995/96, 1999/2000 & 2000/01, Syracuse Crunch; 1996/97, Springfield Falcons; 2003/04, Milwaukee Admirals

AHL Feats: RS Career Rank – 33rd in goals (259); Top 10 RS goals in three seasons; Skated with Calder Cup winning Milwaukee in 2003/04.

	Regular Season					Playoffs			
GP	G	A	Pts.	PIM	GP	G	A	Pts.	PIM
511	259	183	442	557	62	21	22	43	148

138

Travis Scott
Goaltender

Seven seasons (1996/97 <> 2004/05): 1996/97, Worcester IceCats; 1999/2000 & 2000/01, Lowell Lock Monsters; 2001/02 & 2002/03, Manchester Monarchs; 2003/04 & 2004/05, San Antonio Rampage

AHL Feats: RS Career Rank – tied for 12th in shutouts (23).

Regular Season								Playoffs						
GP	W	L	T	MIN	GA	Sho.	GAA	GP	W	L	MIN	GA	Sho.	GAA
321	133	138	23	16528	690	23	2.5	12	3	7	684	31	1	2.72

Peter Sidorkiewicz
Goaltender

Eight seasons (1984/85 <> 1997/98): 1984/85 to 1987/88, Binghamton Whalers; 1993/94 & 1995/96 to 1997/98, Albany River Rats

AHL Feats: RS Career Rank – 15th in wins (179); Harry "Hap" Holmes Memorial Award (lowest team RS GAA) in 1985/86 (#1 RS GAA that season); Second Team All-Star in 1986/87; #1 RS wins in 1984/85; Shares RS one season records for most shootout victories (eight) and most shootout games by a goaltender (13) – both attained in 1986/87.

		Regular Season								Playoffs				
GP	W	L	T	MIN	GA	Sho.	GAA	GP	W	L	MIN	GA	Sho.	GAA
345	179	116	34	19837	1027	17	3.11	47	19	26	11055	144	0	3.17

Cliff Simpson
Center/Left Wing
Eight seasons (1942/43 <> 1951/52): 1942/43 & 1945/46 to 1948/49, Indianapolis Capitols; 1949/50 to 1951/52, St. Louis Flyers

AHL Feats: RS Career Rank – tied for 47th in goals (233); Two All-Star selections – First Team in 1947/48 and Second Team in 1946/47; Top 10 RS goals in five seasons, points in four seasons and assists in two seasons.

		Regular Season						Playoffs		
GP	G	A	Pts.	PIM		GP	G	A	Pts.	PIM
412	233	258	491	116		9	4	4	8	0

John Slaney
Defense

13 seasons (1991/92 <> 2006/07): 1991/92 & 1992/93, Baltimore Skipjacks; 1993/94 & 1994/95, Portland Pirates; 1995/96, Cornwall Aces; 1999/2000 & 2000/01, Wilkes-Barre/Scranton Penguins; 2000/01 to 2006/07, Philadelphia Phantoms

AHL Feats: All-Time RS Leader among defensemen in points (519) since 2005/06 and goals (166) since 2003/04; Other RS Career Rank – tied for 43rd overall in assists (353); Eddie Shore Award (outstanding defenseman) in 2000/01 & 2001/02; Three All-Star selections – First Team in 2000/01 & 2001/02 and Second Team in 2003/04; Top 10 RS assists in one season; Calder Cup winning clubs (two) – Portland in 1993/94 and Philadelphia in 2004/05; RS record for most goals by a defenseman in one season (30) – established in 1999/2000; Shares All-Star Game record for career points (eight); All-Star Game MVP in 2000/01.

	Regular Season					Playoffs			
GP	G	A	Pts.	PIM	GP	G	A	Pts.	PIM
631	166	353	519	340	62	11	28	39	36

142

Gord Smith
Defense

Eight seasons (1972/73 <> 1982/83): 1972/73, 1973/74 & 1981/82, Springfield Indians/Kings; 1974/75 & 1975/76, Richmond Robins; 1978/79, Hershey Bears; 1980/81, New Haven Nighthawks; 1982/83, Maine Mariners

AHL Feats: Eddie Shore Award (outstanding defenseman) in 1973/74; Two All-Star selections – First Team in 1973/74 and Second Team in 1975/76; Top 10 RS assists in one season.

Regular Season						Playoffs				
GP	G	A	Pts.	PIM		GP	G	A	Pts.	PIM
419	25	147	172	632		33	0	9	9	57

Brad Smyth
Right Wing

10 seasons (1994/95 <> 2005/06): 1994/95, Springfield Falcons; 1995/96, Carolina Monarchs; 1997/98 to 2001/02 & 2005/06, Hartford Wolf Pack; 2002/03, Binghamton Senators; 2004/05 & 2005/06, Manchester Monarchs

AHL Feats: RS Career Rank – 10th in goals (326), 26th in points (667) and tied for 50th in assists (341); Elite Achiever – one of seven to lead the circuit in RS goals in two seasons (1995/96 & 2000/01); Les Cunningham Award (RS MVP) in 1995/96; Three All-Star selections – First Team in 1995/96, 2000/01 & 2001/02; #1 RS points (John B. Sollenberger Trophy) in 1995/96; Top 10 RS points in five seasons, goals in four seasons and assists in one season; Skated with Calder Cup winning Hartford in 1999/2000; Shares RS record for most power-play goals in one season (27) – attained in 1995/96.

	Regular Season						Playoffs			
GP	G	A	Pts.	PIM		GP	G	A	Pts.	PIM
610	326	341	667	696		89	46	39	85	75

Bob Solinger
Left Wing

14 seasons (1945/46 <> 1959/60): 1945/46, 1947/48 & 1948/49, Cleveland Barons; 1949/50 to 1955/56, Pittsburgh Hornets; 1956/57 to 1959/60, Hershey Bears

AHL Feats: All-Time PY Leader in points from 1958/59 to 1962/63, goals from 1954/55 to 1961/62 (shared lead in 1960/61 & 1961/62), games played from 1956/57 to 1963/64 and shared the All-Time PY Lead for assists from 1958/59 to 1962/63; RS Career Rank – 43rd in goals (241), 46th in points (590) and 47th in assists (349); Dudley "Red" Garrett Memorial Award (outstanding rookie) in 1947/48; Second Team All-Star in 1952/53; Top 10 RS points, goals and assists in one season; Calder Cup winning clubs (five) – Cleveland in 1947/48, Pittsburgh in 1951/52 & 1954/55 and Hershey in 1957/58 & 1958/59.

		Regular Season					Playoffs		
GP	G	A	Pts.	PIM	GP	G	A	Pts.	PIM
707	241	349	590	435	97	39	53	92	92

Danny Sprout
Defense
Seven seasons: 1943/44 to 1949/50, Cleveland Barons

AHL Feats: All-Time RS Leader among defensemen in points and assists in 1949/50 &
1950/51; Three All-Star selections – Second Team in 1944/45, 1948/49 & 1949/50; Calder Cup
winning clubs (two) – Cleveland in 1944/45 & 1947/48.

	Regular Season					Playoffs			
GP	G	A	Pts.	PIM	GP	G	A	Pts.	PIM
402	42	195	237	246	57	6	27	33	41

146

Art Stratton
Center

12 seasons (1955/56 <> 1974/75): 1955/56 & 1958/59, Cleveland Barons; 1959/60 & 1960/61, Springfield Indians; 1961/62, 1962/63 & 1964/65, Buffalo Bisons; 1963/64, Pittsburgh Hornets; 1971/72 & 1972/73, Tidewater/Virginia Wings; 1973/74, Rochester Americans; 1974/75, Richmond Robins

AHL Feats: RS Career Rank – fifth in assists (555) and 16th in points (766); Les Cunningham Award (RS MVP) in 1964/65 & 1973/74; Four All-Star selections – First Team from 1962/63 to 1964/65 and Second Team in 1973/74; #1 RS assists more times than any other player (four – from 1962/63 to 1964/65 & 1973/74); #1 RS points (John B. Sollenberger Trophy) in 1964/65; Top 10 RS assists in seven seasons, points in six seasons and goals in one season; Calder Cup winning clubs (three) – Springfield in 1959/60 & 1960/61 and Buffalo in 1962/63; RS record for most points and most assists in one game (nine assists/points) – both established on 3/17/63 vs. Pittsburgh @ Buffalo.

	Regular Season					Playoffs			
GP	G	A	Pts.	PIM	GP	G	A	Pts.	PIM
669	211	555	766	430	66	14	41	55	30

Frank Sullivan
Defense

Eight seasons (1951/52 to 1958/59): 1951/52 to 1953/54, Pittsburgh Hornets; 1954/55 to 1957/58, Buffalo Bisons; 1958/59, Springfield Indians

AHL Feats: Three All-Star selections – First Team in 1955/56 and Second Team in 1954/55 & 1956/57; Skated with Calder Cup winning Pittsburgh in 1951/52.

		Regular Season						Playoffs		
GP	G	A	Pts.	PIM		GP	G	A	Pts.	PIM
483	59	246	305	422		41	4	19	23	28

Bill Sweeney
Center

12 seasons (1957/58 to 1968/69): 1957/58, Providence Reds; 1958/59, Buffalo Bisons; 1959/60 to 1967/68, Springfield Indians/Kings; 1968/69, Rochester Americans

AHL HALL OF FAME (2010)

AHL Feats: Elite Achiever – only player to capture the John B. Sollenberger Trophy (RS points leader) in three straight seasons (1960/61 to 1962/63) and one of two players (Peter White) to capture three point-scoring titles; RS Career Rank – eighth in assists (510), 10th in points (804) and 21st in goals (294); Dudley "Red" Garrett Memorial Award (outstanding rookie) in 1957/58; Three All-Star selections – First Team in 1959/60 & 1961/62 and Second Team in 1960/61; #1 RS assists in 1960/61; Top 10 RS assists in eight seasons, points in seven seasons and goals in six seasons; Calder Cup winning clubs (three) – Springfield from 1959/60 to 1961/62.

	Regular Season					Playoffs				
GP	G	A	Pts.	PIM		GP	G	A	Pts.	PIM
695	294	510	804	174		51	23	26	49	8

Joe Szura
Center

Nine seasons (1962/63 <> 1971/72): 1962/63 to 1966/67, Cleveland Barons; 1967/68, Buffalo Bisons; 1969/70 & 1970/71, Providence Reds; 1971/72, Baltimore Clippers

AHL Feats: RS Career Rank – tied for 47th in goals (233); First Team All-Star in 1965/66; Top 10 RS points, goals and assists in two seasons; Skated with Calder Cup winning Cleveland in 1963/64.

Regular Season					Playoffs				
GP	G	A	Pts.	PIM	GP	G	A	Pts.	PIM
608	233	334	567	231	64	24	28	52	53

Fred Thurier
Center

14 seasons (1937/38 <> 1951/52): 1937/38 to 1941/42, Springfield Indians; 1942/43 & 1943/44, Buffalo Bisons; 1945/46 to 1951/52, Cleveland Barons

AHL Feats: All-Time RS Leader in points from 1949/50 to 1959/60, goals from 1950/51 to 1959/60, assists from 1950/51 to 1957/58 and games played from 1949/50 to 1954/55; Current RS Career Rank – 13th in goals (319), 18th in points (744) and 21st in assists (425); All-Time PY Leader in points from 1948/49 to 1958/59, goals from 1949/50 to 1954/55, assists from 1948/49 to 1962/63 (shared assists lead from 1958/59 to 1962/63) and games played from 1950/51 to 1956/57; RS Milestone – first to score 300 goals (3/18/51 @ Indianapolis); Three All-Star selections – First Team in 1940/41 and Second Team in 1941/42 & 1950/51; #1 RS goals in 1940/41; Top 10 RS points and assists in five seasons and goals in three seasons; Calder Cup winning clubs (four) – Buffalo in 1942/43 & 1943/44 and Cleveland in 1947/48 & 1950/51.

	Regular Season					Playoffs			
GP	G	A	Pts.	PIM	GP	G	A	Pts.	PIM
642	319	425	744	367	71	32	53	85	44

Tim Tookey
Center

15 seasons (1980/81 to 1994/95): 1980/81, 1981/82, 1985/86, 1986/87 & 1989/90 to 1993/94, Hershey Bears; 1981/82 & 1982/83, Fredericton Express; 1983/84 & 1984/85, Baltimore Skipjacks; 1987/88 & 1988/89, New Haven Nighthawks; 1994/95, Providence Bruins

AHL HALL OF FAME (2008)

AHL Feats: RS Career Rank – fourth in points (974) and assists (621), ninth in goals (353) and 25th in games played (824); Les Cunningham Award (RS MVP) in 1986/87; Fred T. Hunt Memorial Award (sportsmanship, determination and dedication to hockey) in 1992/93; Jack A. Butterfield Trophy (PY MVP) in 1985/86; Three All-Star selections – First Team in 1986/87 and Second Team in 1985/86 & 1991/92; #1 RS points (John B. Sollenberger Trophy) in 1986/87 and assists in 1985/86 & 1986/87; Top 10 RS assists in five seasons, points in four seasons and goals in one season; The Bears retired his #9 (also retired for Arnie Kullman).

Regular Season					Playoffs				
GP	G	A	Pts.	PIM	GP	G	A	Pts.	PIM
824	353	621	974	689	78	38	44	82	39

Zellio Toppazzini
Right Wing

15 seasons (1948/49 <> 1963/64): 1948/49 to 1950/51, Hershey Bears; 1951/52, Cincinnati Mohawks; 1951/52 to 1958/59 & 1960/61 to 1963/64, Providence Reds

AHL Feats: RS Career Rank – 12th in assists (476), 13th in points (786), 16th in goals (310) and 31st in games played (785); Two All-Star selections – First Team in 1955/56 and Second Team in 1954/55; #1 RS assists in 1954/55 & 1955/56 and points (John B. Sollenberger Trophy) in 1955/56; Top 10 RS assists in four seasons and points and goals in three seasons; Skated with Calder Cup winning Providence in 1955/56.

	Regular Season					Playoffs			
GP	G	A	Pts.	PIM	GP	G	A	Pts.	PIM
785	310	476	786	184	40	16	28	44	8

Jean-Guy Trudel
Left Wing

Five seasons (1999/2000 <> 2007/08): 1999/2000 to 2001/02, Springfield Falcons; 2002/03, Houston Aeros; 2007/08, Peoria Rivermen

AHL Feats: Four All-Star selections – First Team in 2000/01 & 2002/03 and Second Team in 1999/2000 & 2001/02; Top 10 RS assists in three seasons and points and goals in two seasons; Skated with Calder Cup winning Houston in 2002/03.

Regular Season					Playoffs				
GP	G	A	Pts.	PIM	GP	G	A	Pts.	PIM
385	144	250	394	393	26	7	10	17	26

Louis Trudel
Left Wing

Nine seasons (1938/39 <> 1947/48): 1938/39 & 1940/41, New Haven Eagles; 1941/42 & 1942/43, Washington Lions; 1942/43 to 1947/48, Cleveland Barons

AHL Feats: Elite Achiever – one of seven to lead the league in RS goals in two seasons (1941/42 & 1944/45); Four All-Star selections – First Team in 1944/45 and Second Team in 1941/42, 1943/44 & 1945/46; Top 10 RS goals in six seasons, points in four seasons and assists in three seasons; Shared RS mark for most consecutive games with a point (19) – matched record in 1944/45 and the record was surpassed in 1945/46; Calder Cup winning clubs (two) – Cleveland in 1944/45 & 1947/48.

	Regular Season					Playoffs				
GP	G	A	Pts.	PIM		GP	G	A	Pts.	PIM
383	222	261	483	128		43	20	12	32	18

Gilles Villemure
Goaltender

Five seasons (1963/64 <> 1969/70): 1963/64 & 1966/67, Baltimore Clippers; 1967/68 to 1969/70, Buffalo Bisons

AHL Feats: RS Career Rank – tied for ninth in shutouts (24); Les Cunningham Award (RS MVP) in 1968/69 & 1969/70; Harry "Hap" Holmes Memorial Award (lowest RS GAA) in 1968/69 & 1969/70; Three All-Star selections – First Team in 1968/69 & 1969/70 and Second Team in 1966/67; #1 RS shutouts in 1966/67, 1968/69 & 1969/70; Skated with Calder Cup winning Buffalo in 1969/70.

	Regular Season								Playoffs						
GP	W	L	T	MIN	GA	Sho.	GAA	GP	W	L	MIN	GA	Sho.	GAA
300	155	97	43	17688	823	24	3	34	18	15	2051	104	2	3

Peter White
Center

12 seasons (1992/93 <> 2004/05): 1992/93 to 1994/95, Cape Breton Oilers; 1995/96, St. John's Maple Leafs; 1996/97 to 1999/2000 & 2002/03 to 2004/05, Philadelphia Phantoms; 2001/02 & 2002/03, Norfolk Admirals; 2004/05, Utah Grizzlies

AHL Feats: Elite Achiever – one of two players to win the John B. Sollenberger Trophy (RS points leader) on three occasions (1994/95, 1996/97 & 1997/98); RS Career Rank – seventh in assists (533), 14th in points (783), 38th in games played (747) and 40th in goals (250); #1 RS assists in 1994/95 & 1997/98 and goals in 1996/97; Top 10 RS assists in five seasons, points in four seasons and goals in two seasons; Two All-Star selections – Second Team in 1994/95 & 1996/97; Calder Cup winning clubs (three) – Cape Breton in 1992/93 and Philadelphia in 1997/98 & 2004/05; Shares RS record for most consecutive games with an assist (17) – attained in 1993/94.

Regular Season						Playoffs				
GP	G	A	Pts.	PIM		GP	G	A	Pts.	PIM
747	250	533	783	286		92	28	42	70	53

Tommy Williams
Defense

15 seasons (1948/49 <> 1963/64): 1948/49 to 1955/56 & 1960/61 to 1963/64, Cleveland Barons; 1956/57 to 1958/59, Rochester Americans

AHL Feats: RS Career Rank – 27th in games played (822); Five All-Star selections – First Team in 1952/53 & 1956/57 and Second Team in 1951/52, 1953/54 & 1957/58; Calder Cup winning clubs (four) – Cleveland in 1950/51, 1952/53, 1953/54 & 1963/64.

Regular Season					Playoffs				
GP	G	A	Pts.	PIM	GP	G	A	Pts.	PIM
822	22	196	218	237	84	1	19	20	26

Larry Wilson
Center

15 seasons (1950/51 <> 1967/68): 1950/51 & 1951/52, Indianapolis Capitols; 1955/56 to 1967/68, Buffalo Bisons

AHL Feats: RS Career Rank – ninth in assists (492), 12th in points (790), 13th in games played (899) and tied for 19th in goals (298); Two All-Star selections – Second Team in 1955/56 & 1959/60; Top 10 RS points in five seasons, assists in four seasons and goals in two seasons; Skated with Calder Cup winning Buffalo in 1962/63.

	Regular Season					Playoffs				
GP	G	A	Pts.	PIM		GP	G	A	Pts.	PIM
899	298	492	790	543		46	4	13	17	15

Steve Wochy
Right Wing

10 seasons (1945/46 to 1954/55): 1945/46 & 1946/47, Indianapolis Capitols; 1947/48 & 1948/49, Philadelphia Rockets; 1949/50 to 1952/53, Cleveland Barons; 1953/54 & 1954/55, Buffalo Bisons

AHL Feats: RS Career Rank – tied for 35th in goals (253); First Team All-Star in 1951/52; #1 RS goals in 1951/52; Top 10 RS goals in three seasons and points in two seasons; Calder Cup winning clubs (two) – Cleveland in 1950/51 & 1952/53

Regular Season					Playoffs				
GP	G	A	Pts.	PIM	GP	G	A	Pts.	PIM
546	253	262	515	196	24	6	8	14	10

LEGENDARY ADMINISTRATORS
AND HEAD COACHES

John Anderson
Head Coach
Head Coach in seven seasons: 2001/02 to 2007/08, Chicago Wolves

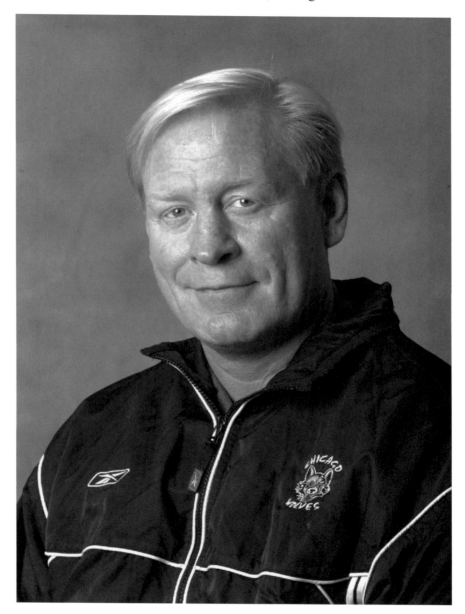

AHL Feats: Two Calder Cup championships with Chicago in 2001/02 & 2007/08; Two division titles; Winning regular seasons (above .500) in seven out of seven campaigns; Qualified for the playoffs in six out of seven seasons.

Regular Season					Playoffs			
G	W	L	T	Pct.	G	W	L	Pct.
560	306	211	43	.585	101	63	38	.624

David Andrews
AHL President/Chief Executive Officer
& General Manager

AHL President/Chief Executive Officer in 16 seasons: 1994/95 to the Present
General Manager in six seasons: 1988/89 to 1993/94, Cape Breton Oilers

AHL Feats: Guided the circuit into unequaled times of prosperity and to record levels of attendance and exposure while expanding its geography across the United States and Canada; Under Andrews' direction, the AHL has become the sole primary development league for all 30 NHL organizations; In 2001, he led one of the largest expansion efforts ever in professional sports by bringing nine new cities into the loop; Andrews was instrumental in re-introducing the All-Star Classic in 1995 after a 35-year absence; Prior to becoming league president/CEO, he was general manager of Cape Breton from 1988/89 to 1993/94 and was named AHL outstanding executive (James C. Hendy Memorial Award) in 1989/90 and won a Calder Cup crown in 1992/93.

Bill Barber
Head Coach

Head Coach in six seasons (1984/85 <> 1999/2000): 1984/85 & 1995/96, Hershey Bears; 1996/97 to 1999/2000, Philadelphia Phantoms

AHL Feats: Calder Cup title with Philadelphia in 1997/98; Two regular season and three division championships; Winning regular seasons (above .500) and made the playoffs in five out of six campaigns.

Regular Season					Playoffs			
G	W	L	T	Pct.	G	W	L	Pct.
382	215	127	40	.615	56	34	22	.607

Bruce Boudreau
Head Coach

Head Coach in nine seasons (1999/2000 to 2007/08): 1999/2000 & 2000/01, Lowell Lock Monsters; 2001/02 to 2004/05, Manchester Monarchs; 2005/06 to 2007/08, Hershey Bears

AHL HALL OF FAME (2009)

AHL Feats: Calder Cup title with Hershey in 2005/06; RS Career Rank – seventh in wins (340) and 10th in games coached (655); One regular season and two division crowns; Winning regular seasons (above .500) in seven out of nine years; Never missed the playoffs.

	Regular Season					Playoffs			
G	W	L	T	Pct.		G	W	L	Pct.
655	340	254	61	.566		71	39	32	.549

Jack Butterfield
Chairman of the AHL Board of Governors
AHL President, General Manager & Head Coach

Chairman of the AHL Board of Governors in 16 seasons: 1994/95 to the Present
AHL President in 28 seasons: 1966/67 to 1993/94
AHL Treasurer in 22 seasons: 1972/73 to 1993/94
General Manager in 10 seasons: 1957/58 to 1966/67, Springfield Indians
Head Coach in one season: 1965/66, Springfield Indians

HOCKEY HALL OF FAME (1980) AND AHL HALL OF FAME (2006)

AHL Feats: Served the longest tenure as Chairman of the AHL Board of Governors (16 seasons) and as league president (28 seasons); Elite Achiever – only general manager to guide his team to three straight Calder Cup crowns – Springfield from 1959/60 to 1961/62; Thomas Ebright Award (outstanding contributions to the AHL) in 1997/98; James C. Hendy Memorial Award (outstanding executive) in 1970/71 & 1983/84; The playoff most valuable player award (the Jack A. Butterfield Trophy), presented since 1983/84, was named in his honor; Credited with keeping the AHL alive during the minor league hockey contraction of the 1970s; He also piloted the Indians for part of 1965/66 as a midseason replacement.

Bill Cook
General Manager & Head Coach

General Manager in three seasons: 1943/44 to 1945/46, Cleveland Barons
Head Coach in six seasons: 1937/38 to 1942/43, Cleveland Barons

HOCKEY HALL OF FAME (1952)

AHL Feats: Two Calder Cup championships with Cleveland in 1938/39 & 1940/41; Two All-Star selections as a head coach – First Team in 1937/38 and Second Team in 1941/42; One regular season and two division titles; Winning regular seasons (above .500) in four out of six campaigns; Qualified for the playoffs in five out of six seasons; Led the Barons to a Calder Cup crown as general manager in 1944/45.

	Regular Season					Playoffs			
G	W	L	T	Pct.		G	W	L	Pct.
326	152	127	47	.538		29	18	11	.621

Fred "Bun" Cook
Head Coach

Head Coach in 19 seasons (1937/38 to 1955/56): 1937/38 to 1942/43, Providence Reds; 1943/44 to 1955/56, Cleveland Barons

HOCKEY HALL OF FAME (1995) AND AHL HALL OF FAME (2007)

AHL Feats: Elite Achiever – most Calder Cup titles (seven – 1937/38, 1939/40, 1944/45, 1947/48, 1950/51, 1952/53 & 1953/54), regular season championships (nine – one in non-division alignment) and first place finishes (10); RS Career Rank – first in wins (636), above .500 seasons (15) and seasons coached (19) and second in games coached (1,171); Seven All-Star selections as head coach – First Team in 1938/39 to 1941/42, 1943/44 & 1944/45 and Second Team in 1942/43; Qualified for the playoffs in 18 out of 19 years

Regular Season					Playoffs			
G	W	L	T	Pct.	G	W	L	Pct.
1171	636	413	122	.595	136	75	61	.551

Johnny Crawford
Head Coach

Head Coach in 10 seasons (1950/51 <> 1965/66): 1950/51 & 1951/52, Hershey Bears; 1955/56 to 1959/60, Providence Reds; 1961/62, Rochester Americans; 1964/65 & 1965/66, Baltimore Clippers

AHL Feats: Calder Cup crown with Providence in 1955/56; RS Career Rank – ninth in wins (333) and games coached (659); Two regular season championships (non-division alignment) and one division title; Winning regular seasons (above .500) and qualified for the playoffs in eight out of 10 years.

Regular Season						Playoffs			
G	W	L	T	Pct.		G	W	L	Pct.
659	333	287	39	.535		42	16	26	.381

Joe Crozier
General Manager & Head Coach

General Manager in seven seasons (1964/65 <> 1971/72): 1964/65 to 1969/70, Rochester Americans; 1971/72, Cincinnati Swords

Head Coach in eight seasons (1963/64 <> 1983/84): 1963/64 to 1967/68 & 1983/84, Rochester Americans; 1971/72, Cincinnati Swords; 1979/80, New Brunswick Hawks;

AHL Feats: Elite Achiever – only general manager/head coach to lead his organization to four Calder Cup finals appearances (Rochester from 1964/65 to 1967/68); Three Calder Cup championships with Rochester in 1964/65, 1965/66 & 1967/68; Two regular season and four division crowns; Never had a club finish below .500 during the regular season or miss the playoffs; Also held the title of vice-president with the Americans in some seasons.

Regular Season					Playoffs			
G	W	L	T	Pct.	G	W	L	Pct.
550	305	199	46	.596	66	39	27	.591

Bill Dineen

General Manager & Head Coach

General Manager in one season: 1989/90, Adirondack Red Wings
Head Coach in six seasons: 1983/84 to 1988/89, Adirondack Red Wings

AHL Feats: Elite Achiever – first bench boss and one of two (Robbie Ftorek) to win the Louis A. R. Pieri Memorial Award (outstanding coach) in consecutive seasons (1984/85 & 1985/86); Two Calder Cup titles with Adirondack in 1985/86 & 1988/89; Two division crowns; Five winning regular seasons (above .500) and playoff appearances in six years.

Regular Season					Playoffs			
G	W	L	T	Pct.	G	W	L	Pct.
480	246	182	52	.567	63	36	27	.571

Pat Egan
Head Coach

Head Coach in eight seasons (1953/54 <> 1964/65): 1953/54 & 1954/55, Providence Reds; 1959/60 to 1964/65, Springfield Indians

AHL Feats: Elite Achiever – only head coach to pilot his team to three Calder Cup championships in a row and three regular season championships in a row (two RS titles in non-division alignment) – he accomplished both with Springfield from 1959/60 to 1961/62; One division crown.

	Regular Season					Playoffs		
G	W	L	T	Pct.	G	W	L	Pct.
564	269	258	37	.510	29	24	5	.828

Robbie Ftorek
General Manager & Head Coach

General Manager in one season: 1989/90, Halifax Citadels
Head Coach in 11 seasons (1985/86 <> 2005/06): 1985/86 to 1987/88, New Haven Nighthawks; 1989/90, Halifax Citadels; 1992/93, Utica Devils; 1993/94 to 1995/96 & 2003/04 to 2005/06, Albany River Rats

UNITED STATES HOCKEY HALL OF FAME (1991)

AHL Feats: Elite Achiever – one of two head coaches to win back-to-back Louis A. R. Pieri Memorial Awards (outstanding coach – 1994/95 & 1995/96); Calder Cup championship with Albany in 1994/95; RS Career Rank – sixth in wins (353) and games coached (743); Two regular season and two division titles; Made playoffs in seven out of 11 campaigns.

	Regular Season					Playoffs			
G	W	L	T	Pct.		G	W	L	Pct.
743	353	310	80	.529		40	19	21	.475

Jack Gordon
General Manager & Head Coach

General Manager in seven seasons: 1960/61 to 1964/65, 1968/69 & 1969/70, Cleveland Barons

Head Coach in eight seasons: 1956/57 to 1961/62, 1968/69 & 1969/70, Cleveland Barons

AHL Feats: Calder Cup championship with Cleveland in 1956/57; Six winning regular seasons (above .500) and seven playoff berths in eight campaigns; One division crown; Also held the title of vice-president with the Barons in some seasons.

	Regular Season					Playoffs			
G	W	L	T	Pct.		G	W	L	Pct.
549	267	234	48	.530		48	21	27	.438

Jim Hendy
Administrator & General Manager
Vice-President in six seasons: 1955/56 to 1960/61, Cleveland Barons
General Manager in 12 seasons: 1949/50 to 1960/61, Cleveland Barons

HOCKEY HALL OF FAME (1968)

AHL Feats: Elite Achiever – one of two general managers (Frank Mathers) with four Calder Cup titles (Cleveland in 1950/51, 1952/53, 1953/54 & 1956/57); The AHL outstanding executive award, instituted in 1961/62, was named in his honor – the James C. Hendy Memorial Award; Author of "The Hockey Guide and Who's Who" from 1932/33 to 1951/52 (popularly known as the "Hendy Guides"), which preserved NHL, AHL and other pro hockey league history.

Al MacNeil
General Manager & Head Coach

General Manager in eight seasons: 1971/72 to 1978/79*, Nova Scotia Voyageurs
Head Coach in seven seasons (1969/70 <> 1976/77): 1969/70, Montreal Voyageurs;
1971/72 to 1976/77, Nova Scotia Voyageurs (* - Title of Director of Player Personnel in 1978/79)

AHL Feats: As general manager/head coach he led Nova Scotia to three Calder Cup titles in
1971/72, 1975/76 & 1976/77; Louis A. R. Pieri Memorial Award (outstanding coach) in 1971/72
& 1976/77; Three regular season (one in non-division alignment) and three division crowns; His
teams always had a winning regular season record (above .500) and qualified for the playoffs.

	Regular Season					Playoffs		
G	W	L	T	Pct.	G	W	L	Pct.
531	304	149	78	.646	69	45	24	.652

Frank Mathers
Administrator, General Manager & Head Coach
President in 18 seasons: 1973/74 to 1990/91, Hershey Bears
General Manager in 24 seasons: 1967/68 to 1990/91, Hershey Bears
Head Coach in 18 seasons: 1956/57 to 1972/73 & 1984/85, Hershey Bears

HOCKEY HALL OF FAME (1992) AND AHL HALL OF FAME (2006)

AHL Feats: Elite Achiever – one of two general managers to win four Calder Cup crowns; All-Time RS Leader – first in games coached (1,256); Other RS Career Rank – second in wins (610); Guided Hershey to six Calder Cup championships – two as a player/head coach (1957/58 & 1958/59), one as a general manager/head coach (1968/69) and three solely as a general manager (1973/74, 1979/80 & 1987/88); James C. Hendy Memorial Award (outstanding executive) in 1976/77 & 1990/91; Louis A. R. Pieri Memorial Award (outstanding coach) in 1968/69; One regular season title (non-division alignment) and three division titles; In 18 campaigns behind the bench he only had two regular seasons where his outfit finished below .500 and missed the playoffs; Named Honorary Life member of the AHL Board of Governors in 1994 (he was an Honorary Governor and Presidential Consultant in 1992/93 & 1993/94).

| | Regular Season | | | | | Playoffs | | | |
G	W	L	T	Pct.		G	W	L	Pct.
1256	610	512	134	.539		128	60	68	.469

Bob McCammon
Head Coach
Head Coach in five seasons: 1977/78 to 1981/82, Maine Mariners

AHL Feats: Elite Achiever – only head coach to guide a club to a Calder Cup crown during its first two seasons of existence (Maine in 1977/78 & 1978/79); Louis A. R. Pieri Memorial Award (outstanding coach) in 1977/78 & 1980/81; Two regular season and three division championships; His squads never had a losing regular season (below .500) or missed the playoffs.

| | Regular Season | | | | | | Playoffs | | | |
G	W	L	T	Pct.		G	W	L	Pct.
400	221	132	47	.611		58	33	25	.569

John Paddock
Head Coach

Head Coach in 15 seasons (1981/82 <> 2008/09): 1981/82, 1983/84 & 1984/85, Maine Mariners; 1985/86 to 1988/89, Hershey Bears; 1990/91, Binghamton Rangers; 1999/2000 to 2001/02, Hartford Wolf Pack; 2002/03 to 2004/05, Binghamton Senators; 2008/09, Philadelphia Phantoms

AHL HALL OF FAME (2010)

AHL Feats: Elite Achiever – only head coach in circuit history to win the Calder Cup with three different organizations (Maine in 1983/84, Hershey in 1987/88 and Hartford in 1999/2000); RS Career Rank – third in wins (585) and games coached (1,107); Louis A. R. Pieri Memorial Award (outstanding coach) in 1987/88 (shared); Three regular season and six division titles; Had just one sub-.500 regular season in 15 campaigns and never missed the playoffs.

	Regular Season					Playoffs			
G	W	L	T	Pct.		G	W	L	Pct.
1107	585	424	98	.573		149	82	67	.550

Louis A. R. Pieri
Administrator & General Manager

Owner/President in 28 seasons: 1939/40 to 1966/67, Providence Reds

General Manager/Manager for many seasons: 1939/40*, 1940s*, 1948/49 to 1953/54, Providence Reds (* - Official title was not general manager, but performed general manager duties; Uncertain if Pieri was general manager/manager in some years in early 1940s)

AHL HALL OF FAME (2009)

AHL Feats: General Manager* of Calder Cup winning Providence clubs of 1937/38, 1939/40 & 1948/49; James C. Hendy Memorial Award (outstanding executive) in 1966/67; Owned the Reds from 1939/40 until his death in the summer of 1967; The AHL initiated an annual outstanding coach award in his name (the Louis A. R. Pieri Memorial Award) starting with the 1967/68 season.

Maurice Podoloff
League Founder & First League President
AHL President in 16 seasons: 1936/37 to 1951/52

AHL Feats: President of the league during its first 16 seasons from 1936/37 to 1951/52; Helped establish the AHL from the amalgamation of the Canadian-American Hockey League (CAHL) and the International Hockey League (IHL); Successfully guided the loop during the Great Depression and World War II.

Terry Reardon
Administrator, General Manager & Head Coach

Owner in one season: 1975/76, Baltimore Clippers
Vice-President in two seasons: 1973/74 & 1974/75, Baltimore Clippers
General Manager in 21 seasons (1955/56 to 1975/76): 1955/56 to 1961/62, Providence Reds; 1962/63 to 1975/76, Baltimore Clippers
Head Coach in 15 seasons (1947/48 <> 1975/76): 1947/48 to 1952/53, Providence Reds; 1965/66 to 1967/68 & 1970/71 to 1975/76, Baltimore Clippers

AHL Feats: Won a Calder Cup championship with Providence in 1948/49; RS Career Rank – fifth in wins (362) and games coached (794); Louis A. R. Pieri Memorial Award (outstanding coach) in 1970/71; Two regular season and five division crowns; His squads made the playoffs in eight of 14* campaigns (* - Baltimore withdrew from the AHL prior to 1974/75 postseason).

	Regular Season					Playoffs			
G	W	L	T	Pct.		G	W	L	Pct.
794	362	359	73	.502		71	33	38	.465

Jimmy Roberts
General Manager & Head Coach

General Manager in two seasons: 1994/95 & 1995/96, Worcester IceCats
Head Coach in five seasons (1988/89 <> 1995/96): 1988/89 to 1990/91, Springfield
Indians; 1994/95 & 1995/96, Worcester IceCats

AHL Feats: Elite Achiever – the last head coach to pilot his team to back-to-back Calder Cup
titles (Springfield in 1989/90 & 1990/91); Louis A. R. Pieri Memorial Award (outstanding coach)
in 1989/90; One division crown; Qualified for the playoffs in three out of five campaigns.

	Regular Season					Playoffs		
G	W	L	T	Pct.	G	W	L	Pct.
400	173	186	41	.484	40	25	15	.625

Eddie Shore
Administrator, General Manager & Head Coach

Owner/President in 30 seasons: 1939/40 to 1941/42, 1946/47 to 1950/51 & 1954/55 to 1975/76, Springfield Indians/Kings; 1951/52 to 1953/54, Syracuse Warriors

General Manager/Manager in 25 seasons: 1939/40 to 1956/57, Springfield Indians; 1942/43 to 1944/45, Buffalo Bisons; 1945/46, New Haven Eagles; 1951/52 to 1953/54, Syracuse Warriors

Head Coach in one season: 1954/55, Springfield Indians

(Note: During the Springfield Kings era [1967/68 to 1974/75*] Shore leased his AHL franchise to the Los Angeles Kings, while maintaining ownership of the franchise; He was the AHL Kings representative on the circuit's board of governors; Shore changed the club's name back to Indians midway through 1974/75)

HOCKEY HALL OF FAME (1947) AND AHL HALL OF FAME (2006)

AHL Feats: Owned AHL clubs in Springfield and Syracuse; As an owner with Springfield and as a general manager with Buffalo his outfits captured seven Calder Cup championships – from 1959/60 to 1961/62, 1970/71 & 1974/75 with the Indians/Kings and in 1942/43 & 1943/44 with the Bisons; James C. Hendy Memorial Award (outstanding executive) in 1969/70; Head Coach of the Indians in 1954/55 and went 32-29-3 (.523); In 1958/59, the AHL inaugurated the Eddie Shore Award to be given annually to the player chosen as the outstanding defenseman; Given the title Honorary Governor on the league's board of governors in 1977; The Springfield Falcons retired the #2 in his honor (his #2 was previously retired by the Boston Bruins).

Al Sutphin
League Founder, Administrator & General Manager

Owner/President in 13 seasons: 1936/37 to 1948/49, Cleveland Barons/Falcons
General Manager*/Manager in seven seasons: 1936/37 to 1942/43, Cleveland
Barons/Falcons (* – Never had official title of general manager, but performed general manager duties)

AHL Feats: Made the Barons into the dominant force in the AHL; Helped keep the circuit afloat during World War II; When other organizations got into financial trouble he would bail them out; It was his undying loyalty to his fellow AHL owners that led him to turn down the NHL owners' invitation to join their league in the early 1940s; General Manager* of three Calder Cup winning teams with Cleveland in 1938/39, 1940/41 & 1947/48.

John Van Boxmeer
Head Coach

Head Coach in nine seasons: 1984/85 to 1989/90 & 1992/93 to 1994/95, Rochester Americans

AHL Feats: Won a Calder Cup title with Rochester in 1986/87; RS Career Rank – eighth in wins (337) and games coached (695); Two division crowns; Winning regular seasons (above .500) in six out of nine campaigns; Postseason berths in seven out of nine campaigns.

Regular Season					Playoffs			
G	W	L	T	Pct.	G	W	L	Pct.
695	337	283	75	.539	73	36	37	.493

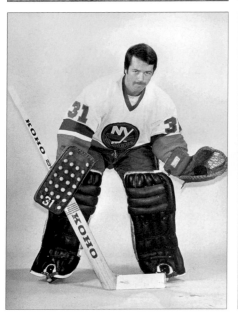

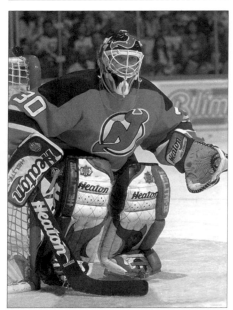

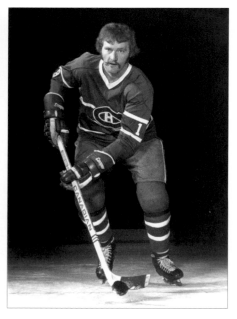

Sid Abel
Center/Left Wing

Two AHL seasons (1938/39 & 1939/40): 1938/39, Pittsburgh Hornets; 1939/40, Indianapolis Capitols

14 NHL seasons (1938/39 <> 1953/54): 1938/39 to 1942/43 & 1945/46 to 1951/52, Detroit Red Wings; 1952/53 & 1953/54, Chicago Black Hawks

NHL

	Regular Season					Playoffs			
GP	G	A	Pts.	PIM	GP	G	A	Pts.	PIM
612	189	283	472	376	97	28	30	58	79

NHL Feats: Hockey Hall of Fame (1969); Hart Memorial Trophy (RS MVP) in 1948/49; Four All-Star selections – First Team in 1948/49 & 1949/50 and Second Team in 1941/42 & 1950/51; #1 RS goals in 1948/49; Top 10 RS assists in eight seasons, points in five seasons and goals in three seasons; Stanley Cup winning clubs (three) – Detroit in 1942/43, 1949/50 & 1951/52; The Red Wings retired his #12.

AHL

	Regular Season					Playoffs			
GP	G	A	Pts.	PIM	GP	G	A	Pts.	PIM
62	29	35	64	37	--	--	--	---	---

AHL Feats: Top 10 RS goals in one season.

George Armstrong
Center/Right Wing

Two AHL seasons: 1950/51 & 1951/52, Pittsburgh Hornets
21 NHL seasons: 1949/50 & 1951/52 to 1970/71, Toronto Maple Leafs

NHL

	Regular Season					Playoffs			
GP	G	A	Pts.	PIM	GP	G	A	Pts.	PIM
1187	296	417	713	721	110	26	34	60	52

NHL Feats: Hockey Hall of Fame (1975); Stanley Cup winning clubs (four) – Toronto from 1961/62 to 1963/64 & 1966/67.

AHL

	Regular Season					Playoffs			
GP	G	A	Pts.	PIM	GP	G	A	Pts.	PIM
121	45	62	107	111	13	4	9	13	6

AHL Feats: Top 10 RS goals in one season; Skated with Calder Cup winning Pittsburgh in 1951/52.

Bobby Bauer
Right Wing

One AHL season: 1936/37, Providence Reds
Nine NHL seasons: 1936/37 to 1941/42, 1945/46, 1946/47 & 1951/52, Boston Bruins

NHL

Regular Season					Playoffs				
GP	G	A	Pts.	PIM	GP	G	A	Pts.	PIM
327	123	137	260	36	48	11	8	19	6

NHL Feats: Hockey Hall of Fame (1996); Lady Byng Memorial Trophy (most gentlemanly player) in 1939/40, 1940/41 & 1946/47; Four All-Star selections – Second Team in 1938/39 to 1940/41 & 1946/47; Top 10 RS goals in four seasons, points in three seasons and assists in two seasons; Stanley Cup winning clubs (two) – Boston in 1938/39 & 1940/41.

AHL

Regular Season					Playoffs				
GP	G	A	Pts.	PIM	GP	G	A	Pts.	PIM
44	14	4	18	4	2	0	1	1	0

Johnny Bower
Goaltender

11 AHL seasons (1945/46 <> 1957/58): 1945/46 to 1952/53 & 1957/58, Cleveland Barons; 1945/46, 1955/56 & 1956/57, Providence Reds

15 NHL seasons (1953/54 <> 1969/70): 1953/54, 1954/55 & 1956/57, New York Rangers; 1958/59 to 1969/70, Toronto Maple Leafs

NHL

		Regular Season								Playoffs				
GP	W	L	T	MIN	GA	Sho.	GAA	GP	W	L	MIN	GA	Sho.	GAA
552	250	195	90	32016	1340	37	2.51	74	35	34	4378	180	5	2.47

NHL Feats: Hockey Hall of Fame (1976); Vezina Trophy (outstanding goaltender) in '61 & '65 (shared); First Team All-Star in '61; Stanley Cup winning clubs (four) – Toronto from '62 to '64 & '67.

AHL

		Regular Season								Playoffs				
GP	W	L	T	MIN	GA	Sho.	GAA	GP	W	L	MIN	GA	Sho.	GAA
592	359	174	57	35799	1684	45	2.82	55	31	24	3465	158	4	2.74

AHL Feats: AHL Hall of Fame (2006); Les Cunningham Award (RS MVP) from '56 to '58; Harry "Hap" Holmes Memorial Award (lowest RS GAA) in '52, '57 & '58; Six All-Star selections – First Team in '52, '53 & '56 to '58 and Second Team in '51; Calder Cup winning clubs (four) – Cleveland in '48, '51 & '53 and Providence in '56.

Frank Brimsek

Goaltender

Two AHL seasons (1937/38 & 1938/39): 1937/38 & 1938/39, Providence Reds; 1937/38, New Haven Eagles

10 NHL seasons (1938/39 <> 1949/50): 1938/39 to 1942/43 & 1945/46 to 1948/49, Boston Bruins; 1949/50, Chicago Black Hawks

NHL

	Regular Season								Playoffs					
GP	W	L	T	MIN	GA	Sho.	GAA	GP	W	L	MIN	GA	Sho.	GAA
514	252	182	80	31210	1404	40	2.70	68	32	36	4395	186	2	2.54

NHL Feats: Hockey Hall of Fame (1966); United States Hockey Hall of Fame (1973); Vezina Trophy (outstanding goaltender) in 1938/39 & 1941/42; Calder Memorial Trophy (outstanding rookie) in 1938/39; Eight All-Star selections – First Team in 1938/39 & 1941/42 and Second Team in 1939/40, 1940/41, 1942/43 & 1945/46 to 1947/48; #1 RS goals-against average in 1938/39 & 1941/42, wins in 1938/39 & 1939/40 and shutouts in 1938/39 & 1940/41; Stanley Cup winning clubs (two) – Boston in 1938/39 & 1940/41.

AHL

	Regular Season								Playoffs					
GP	W	L	T	MIN	GA	Sho.	GAA	GP	W	L	MIN	GA	Sho.	GAA
57	30	18	9	3520	104	5	1.77	8	5	3	608	19	0	1.88

AHL Feats: His goals-against average of 1.79 in 1937/38 was the circuit's one season record for almost 70 seasons – it was not broken until 2003/04; First Team All-Star in 1937/38; #1 RS goals-against average in 1937/38; Skated with Calder Cup winning Providence in 1937/38.

Martin Brodeur
Goaltender

One AHL season: 1992/93, Utica Devils
17 NHL seasons: 1991/92, 1993/94 to 2003/04 & 2005/06 to 2009/10, New Jersey Devils

NHL

				Regular Season							Playoffs			
GP	W	L	T	MIN	GA	Sho.	GAA	GP	W	L	MIN	GA	Sho.	GAA
1076	602	324	135	63521	2340	110	2.21	181	99	81	11248	376	23	2.01

NHL Feats: All-Time RS Leader in wins (602) – since 2008/09 – and shutouts (110), games in goal (1,076) and minutes played (63,521) – since 2009/10; Vezina Trophy (outstanding goaltender) in '03, '04, '07 & '08; William M. Jennings Trophy (lowest RS team GAA) in '97 (shared, but #1 RS GAA), '98, '03 (shared), '04 & '10; Calder Memorial Trophy (outstanding rookie) in '94; Seven All-Star selections – First Team in '03, '04 & '07 and Second Team in '97, '98, '06 & '08; Stanley Cup winning clubs (three) – New Jersey in '95, '00 & '03.

AHL

				Regular Season							Playoffs			
GP	W	L	T	MIN	GA	Sho.	GAA	GP	W	L	MIN	GA	Sho.	GAA
32	14	13	5	1952	131	0	4.03	4	1	3	258	18	0	4.19

AHL Feats: Shares RS record for most assists by a goaltender in one game (three) – attained on 1/23/93 @ Adirondack).

Gerry Cheevers
Goaltender

Four AHL seasons (1961/62 to 1964/65): 1961/62, Pittsburgh Hornets; 1961/62 to 1964/65, Rochester Americans

13 NHL seasons (1961/62 <> 1979/80): 1961/62, Toronto Maple Leafs; 1965/66, 1971/72 & 1975/76 to 1979/80, Boston Bruins

NHL

	Regular Season							Playoffs						
GP	W	L	T	MIN	GA	Sho.	GAA	GP	W	L	MIN	GA	Sho.	GAA
418	230	102	74	24394	1174	26	2.89	88	53	34	5396	242	8	2.69

NHL Feats: Hockey Hall of Fame (1985); RS record for longest undefeated streak by a goaltender in one season (32 games – 24-0-8) – established in 1971/72; Stanley Cup winning clubs (three) – Toronto in 1961/62 and Boston in 1969/70 & 1971/72.

AHL

	Regular Season							Playoffs						
GP	W	L	T	MIN	GA	Sho.	GAA	GP	W	L	MIN	GA	Sho.	GAA
181	104	66	10	10899	547	10	3.01	14	10	4	855	40	0	2.81

AHL Feats: Harry "Hap" Holmes Memorial Award (lowest RS GAA) in 1964/65; First Team All-Star in 1964/65; #1 RS wins in 1963/64 & 1964/65 and shutouts in 1964/65; RS record for most games won by a goaltender in one season (48) – set in 1964/65; Skated with Calder Cup winning Rochester in 1964/65.

Ken Dryden
Goaltender

One AHL season: 1970/71, Montreal Voyageurs
Eight NHL seasons: 1970/71 to 1972/73 & 1974/75 to 1978/79, Montreal Canadiens

NHL

	Regular Season								Playoffs						
GP	W	L	T	MIN	GA	Sho.	GAA	GP	W	L	MIN	GA	Sho.	GAA
397	258	57	74	23352	870	46	2.24	112	80	32	6846	274	10	2.40

NHL Feats: Hockey Hall of Fame (1983); Vezina Trophy (outstanding goaltender) in '73 & '76 to '79 (the last three shared); Calder Memorial Trophy (outstanding rookie) in '72; Conn Smythe Trophy (PY MVP) in '71; Six All-Star selections – First Team in '73 & '76 to '79 and Second Team in '72; #1 RS goals-against average in '73, '76, '78 & '79, wins in '72, '73, '76 & '77 and shutouts in '73, '76, '77 & '79; Stanley Cup winning clubs (six) – Montreal in '71, '73 & '76 to '79; The Canadiens retired his #29.

AHL

	Regular Season								Playoffs						
GP	W	L	T	MIN	GA	Sho.	GAA	GP	W	L	MIN	GA	Sho.	GAA
33	16	7	8	1899	84	3	2.68	--	--	--	---	--	---	---

Eddie Giacomin
Goaltender

Seven AHL seasons (1959/60 to 1965/66): 1959/60 to 1964/65, Providence Reds; 1965/66, Baltimore Clippers
13 NHL seasons (1965/66 to 1977/78): 1965/66 to 1975/76, New York Rangers; 1975/76 to 1977/78, Detroit Red Wings

NHL

	Regular Season								Playoffs					
GP	W	L	T	MIN	GA	Sho.	GAA	GP	W	L	MIN	GA	Sho.	GAA
609	289	209	96	35633	1672	54	2.82	65	29	35	3838	180	1	2.81

NHL Feats: Hockey Hall of Fame (1987); Vezina Trophy (outstanding goaltender) in 1970/71 (shared); Five All-Star selections – First Team in 1966/67 & 1970/71 and Second Team in 1967/68 to 1969/70; #1 RS wins from 1966/67 to 1968/69 and shutouts in 1966/67, 1967/68 & 1970/71; The Rangers retired his #1.

AHL

	Regular Season								Playoffs					
GP	W	L	T	MIN	GA	Sho.	GAA	GP	W	L	MIN	GA	Sho.	GAA
258	112	133	10	15397	912	12	3.55	9	3	6	479	43	0	5.39

AHL Feats: #1 RS shutouts in 1963/64.

Glenn Hall
Goaltender

One AHL season: 1951/52, Indianapolis Capitols
18 NHL seasons (1952/53 <> 1970/71): 1952/53 & 1954/55 to 1956/57, Detroit Red Wings; 1957/58 to 1966/67, Chicago Black Hawks; 1967/68 to 1970/71, St. Louis Blues

NHL

	Regular Season								Playoffs						
GP	W	L	T	MIN	GA	Sho.	GAA		GP	W	L	MIN	GA	Sho.	GAA
906	407	326	163	53484	2222	84	2.49		115	49	65	6899	320	6	2.78

NHL Feats: Hockey Hall of Fame (1975); Vezina Trophy (outstanding goaltender) in '63, '67 & '69 (the last two shared); Calder Memorial Trophy (outstanding rookie) in '56; Conn Smythe Trophy (PY MVP) in '68; 11 All-Star selections – First Team in '57, '58, '60, '63, '64, '66 & '69 and Second Team in '56, '61, '62 & '67; RS record for most consecutive complete games by a goaltender (502) – streak was from 1955/56 to 1962/63; Stanley Cup winning clubs (two) – Detroit in '55 and Chicago in '61; The Black Hawks retired his #1.

AHL

	Regular Season								Playoffs						
GP	W	L	T	MIN	GA	Sho.	GAA		GP	W	L	MIN	GA	Sho.	GAA
68	22	40	6	4190	272	0	3.89		--	--	--	---	--	---	---

Bryan Hextall Sr.
Right Wing

Two AHL seasons (1936/37 & 1948/49): 1936/37, Philadelphia Ramblers; 1948/49, Cleveland Barons; 1948/49, Washington Lions
11 NHL seasons: 1936/37 to 1943/44 & 1945/46 to 1947/48, New York Rangers

NHL

	Regular Season					Playoffs			
GP	G	A	Pts.	PIM	GP	G	A	Pts.	PIM
449	187	175	362	227	37	8	9	17	19

NHL Feats: Hockey Hall of Fame (1969); Art Ross Trophy (RS points leader) in 1941/42; #1 RS points in 1941/42 and goals in 1939/40 & 1940/41; Top 10 RS goals in six seasons, points in four seasons and assists in one season; Four All-Star selections – First Team from 1939/40 to 1941/42 and Second Team in 1942/43; Skated with the Stanley Cup winning Rangers in 1939/40.

AHL

	Regular Season					Playoffs			
GP	G	A	Pts.	PIM	GP	G	A	Pts.	PIM
107	45	48	93	56	6	2	4	6	6

AHL Feats: #1 RS goals in 1936/37; Top 10 RS assists in two seasons and points and goals in one season.

Tim Horton
Defense

Three AHL seasons: 1949/50 to 1951/52, Pittsburgh Hornets

24 NHL seasons (1949/50 <> 1973/74): 1949/50 & 1951/52 to 1969/70, Toronto Maple Leafs; 1969/70 & 1970/71, New York Rangers; 1971/72, Pittsburgh Penguins; 1972/73 & 1973/74, Buffalo Sabres

NHL

	Regular Season					Playoffs			
GP	G	A	Pts.	PIM	GP	G	A	Pts.	PIM
1446	115	403	518	1611	126	11	39	50	183

NHL Feats: Hockey Hall of Fame (1977); RS Career Rank – tied for third in seasons played (24); Six All-Star selections – First Team in 1963/64, 1967/68 & 1968/69 and Second Team in 1953/54, 1962/63 & 1966/67; Stanley Cup winning clubs (four) – Toronto from 1961/62 to 1963/64 & 1966/67; Buffalo retired his #2.

AHL

	Regular Season					Playoffs			
GP	G	A	Pts.	PIM	GP	G	A	Pts.	PIM
192	25	63	88	358	24	1	12	13	32

AHL Feats: First Team All-Star in 1951/52; Skated with Calder Cup winning Pittsburgh in 1951/52.

Brett Hull
Right Wing

One AHL season: 1986/87, Moncton Golden Flames
20 NHL seasons (1985/86 <> 2005/06): 1985/86 to 1987/88, Calgary Flames; 1987/88 to 1997/98, St. Louis Blues; 1998/99 to 2000/01, Dallas Stars; 2001/02 to 2003/04, Detroit Red Wings; 2005/06, Phoenix Coyotes

NHL

| | Regular Season | | | | | Playoffs | | | |
GP	G	A	Pts.	PIM	GP	G	A	Pts.	PIM
1269	741	650	1391	458	202	103	87	190	73

NHL Feats: Hockey Hall of Fame (2009); United States Hockey Hall of Fame (2008); RS Career Rank – third in goals (741), 21st in points (1,391) and 57th in assists (650); Hart Memorial Trophy (RS MVP) in '91; Lady Byng Memorial Trophy (most gentlemanly player) in '90; Lester B. Pearson Award (NHL Players' Association MVP) in '91; Three All-Star selections – First Team from '90 to '92; #1 RS goals from '90 to '92; Stanley Cup winning clubs (two) – Dallas in '99 and Detroit in '02; St. Louis retired his #16.

AHL

| | Regular Season | | | | | Playoffs | | | |
GP	G	A	Pts.	PIM	GP	G	A	Pts.	PIM
67	50	42	92	16	3	2	2	4	2

AHL Feats: Tim Horton Trophy (Canadian-based team outstanding player – W) in 1986/87; Dudley "Red" Garrett Memorial Award (outstanding rookie) in 1986/87; First Team All-Star in 1986/87; Top 10 RS goals in one season.

Tom Johnson
Defense

Two AHL seasons: 1948/49 & 1949/50, Buffalo Bisons
17 NHL seasons (1947/48 <> 1964/65): 1947/48 & 1949/50 to 1962/63, Montreal Canadiens; 1963/64 & 1964/65, Boston Bruins

NHL

	Regular Season					Playoffs			
GP	G	A	Pts.	PIM	GP	G	A	Pts.	PIM
978	51	213	264	960	111	8	15	23	109

NHL Feats: Hockey Hall of Fame (1970); James Norris Memorial Trophy (outstanding defenseman) in 1958/59; Two All-Star selections – First Team in 1958/59 and Second Team in 1955/56; Stanley Cup winning clubs (six) – Montreal in 1952/53 & 1955/56 to 1959/60.

AHL

	Regular Season					Playoffs			
GP	G	A	Pts.	PIM	GP	G	A	Pts.	PIM
126	11	37	48	122	5	0	0	0	20

Guy Lapointe
Defense

One AHL season: 1969/70, Montreal Voyageurs
16 NHL seasons (1968/69 to 1983/84): 1968/69 to 1981/82, Montreal Canadiens; 1981/82 & 1982/83, St. Louis Blues; 1983/84, Boston Bruins

NHL

	Regular Season					Playoffs			
GP	G	A	Pts.	PIM	GP	G	A	Pts.	PIM
884	171	451	622	893	123	26	44	70	138

NHL Feats: Hockey Hall of Fame (1993); Four All-Star selections – First Team in 1972/73 and Second Team from 1974/75 to 1976/77; Stanley Cup winning clubs (seven) – Montreal in 1968/69, 1970/71, 1972/73 & 1975/76 to 1978/79.

AHL

	Regular Season					Playoffs			
GP	G	A	Pts.	PIM	GP	G	A	Pts.	PIM
57	8	30	38	92	8	3	5	8	6

AHL Feats: First Team All-Star in 1969/70.

Harry Lumley
Goaltender

Five AHL seasons (1943/44 <> 1958/59): 1943/44 & 1944/45, Indianapolis Capitols; 1956/57 & 1957/58, Buffalo Bisons; 1958/59, Providence Reds
16 NHL seasons (1943/44 <> 1959/60): 1943/44 to 1949/50, Detroit Red Wings; 1943/44, New York Rangers; 1950/51 & 1951/52, Chicago Black Hawks; 1952/53 to 1955/56, Toronto Maple Leafs; 1957/58 to 1959/60, Boston Bruins

NHL

	Regular Season							Playoffs						
GP	W	L	T	MIN	GA	Sho.	GAA	GP	W	L	MIN	GA	Sho.	GAA
803	330	329	142	48044	2206	71	2.75	76	29	47	4778	198	7	2.49

NHL Feats: Hockey Hall of Fame (1980); Vezina Trophy (outstanding goaltender) in 1953/54; Two All-Star Selections – First Team in 1953/54 & 1954/55; #1 RS shutouts in 1947/48, 1952/53 & 1953/54, goals-against average in 1953/54 & 1954/55 and wins in 1948/49 & 1949/50; Skated with Stanley Cup winning Detroit in 1949/50.

AHL

	Regular Season							Playoffs						
GP	W	L	T	MIN	GA	Sho.	GAA	GP	W	L	MIN	GA	Sho.	GAA
211	89	97	25	12669	728	7	3.45	5	1	4	300	18	0	3.60

AHL Feats: Second Team All-Star in 1956/57; RS record for most tie games by a goaltender in one season (15) – established in 1943/44.

Pierre Pilote
Defense

Five AHL seasons: 1951/52 to 1955/56, Buffalo Bisons
14 NHL seasons (1955/56 to 1968/69): 1955/56 to 1967/68, Chicago Black Hawks; 1968/69, Toronto Maple Leafs

NHL

	Regular Season					Playoffs			
GP	G	A	Pts.	PIM	GP	G	A	Pts.	PIM
890	80	418	498	1251	86	8	53	61	102

NHL Feats: Hockey Hall of Fame (1975); James Norris Memorial Trophy (outstanding defenseman) from 1962/63 to 1964/65; Eight All-Star selections – First Team from 1962/63 to 1966/67 and Second Team from 1959/60 to 1961/62; Top 10 RS assists in three seasons and points in one season; Skated with Stanley Cup winning Chicago in 1960/61; The Black Hawks retired his #3 (also retired for Keith Magnuson).

AHL

	Regular Season					Playoffs			
GP	G	A	Pts.	PIM	GP	G	A	Pts.	PIM
236	14	82	96	435	18	0	6	6	28

Jacques Plante
Goaltender

Three AHL seasons (1952/53 <> 1964/65): 1952/53 & 1953/54, Buffalo Bisons; 1964/65, Baltimore Clippers

18 NHL seasons (1952/53 <> 1972/73): 1952/53 to 1962/63, Montreal Canadiens; 1963/64 & 1964/65, New York Rangers; 1968/69 & 1969/70, St. Louis Blues; 1970/71 to 1972/73, Toronto Maple Leafs; 1972/73, Boston Bruins

NHL

	Regular Season								Playoffs						
GP	W	L	T	MIN	GA	Sho.	GAA	GP	W	L	MIN	GA	Sho.	GAA
837	437	246	145	49533	1964	82	2.38	112	71	36	6651	237	14	2.14

NHL Feats: Hockey Hall of Fame (1978); Hart Memorial Trophy (RS MVP) in '62; Vezina Trophy (outstanding goaltender) from '56 to '60, '62 & '69 (shared); Seven All-Star selections – First Team in '56, '59 & '62 and Second Team in '57, '58, '60 & '71; #1 RS goals-against average from '56 to '60, '62, '63, '69 & '71, wins in '56, '58 to '60 & '62 and shutouts in '57 to '59 & '63; Stanley Cup winning clubs (six) – Montreal in '53 & '56 to '60; The Canadiens retired his #1.

AHL

	Regular Season								Playoffs						
GP	W	L	T	MIN	GA	Sho.	GAA	GP	W	L	MIN	GA	Sho.	GAA
105	51	45	8	6388	313	6	2.94	5	2	3	315	14	1	2.67

AHL Feats: #1 RS goals-against average in 1953/54 (Note: Gil Mayer was awarded the Harry "Hap" Holmes Memorial Award [lowest RS GAA] that season. No official reason why was given in the official AHL Red Book of 1953/54, but Mayer played substantially more games than Plante).

Chuck Rayner
Goaltender

Three AHL seasons (1940/41 <> 1947/48):1940/41 & 1941/42, Springfield Indians; 1947/48, New Haven Ramblers
10 NHL seasons (1940/41 <> 1952/53):1940/41 & 1941/42, New York/Brooklyn Americans; 1945/46 to 1952/53, New York Rangers

NHL

		Regular Season								Playoffs				
GP	W	L	T	MIN	GA	Sho.	GAA	GP	W	L	MIN	GA	Sho.	GAA
424	138	208	77	25491	1294	25	3.05	18	9	9	1135	46	1	2.43

NHL Feats: Hockey Hall of Fame (1973); Hart Memorial Trophy (RS MVP) in 1949/50; #1 RS shutouts in 1946/47; Three All-Star selections – Second Team from 1948/49 to 1950/51.

AHL

		Regular Season								Playoffs				
GP	W	L	T	MIN	GA	Sho.	GAA	GP	W	L	MIN	GA	Sho.	GAA
53	25	19	8	3240	131	6	2.43	--	--	--	---	--	---	---

AHL Feats: Second Team All-Star in 1940/41; #1 RS goals-against average and shutouts in 1940/41.

Larry Robinson
Defense

Two AHL seasons: 1971/72 & 1972/73, Nova Scotia Voyageurs
20 NHL seasons (1972/73 to 1991/92): 1972/73 to 1988/89, Montreal Canadiens; 1989/90 to 1991/92, Los Angeles Kings

NHL

	Regular Season					Playoffs			
GP	G	A	Pts.	PIM	GP	G	A	Pts.	PIM
1384	208	750	958	793	227	28	116	144	211

NHL Feats: Hockey Hall of Fame (1995); RS Career Rank – 39th in assists (750) and 83rd in points (958); James Norris Memorial Trophy (outstanding defenseman) in 1976/77 & 1979/80; Conn Smythe Trophy (PY MVP) in 1977/78; Six All-Star selections – First Team in 1976/77, 1978/79 & 1979/80 and Second Team in 1977/78, 1980/81 & 1985/86; Top 10 RS assists in three seasons; Stanley Cup winning clubs (six) – Montreal in 1972/73, 1975/76 to 1978/79 & 1985/86; The Canadiens retired his #19.

AHL

	Regular Season					Playoffs			
GP	G	A	Pts.	PIM	GP	G	A	Pts.	PIM
112	16	47	63	87	15	2	10	12	31

AHL Feats: Skated with Calder Cup winning Nova Scotia in 1971/72.

Terry Sawchuk
Goaltender

Two AHL seasons: 1948/49 & 1949/50, Indianapolis Capitols
21 NHL seasons (1949/50 to 1969/70): 1949/50 to 1954/55, 1957/58 to 1963/64 & 1968/69, Detroit Red Wings; 1955/56 & 1956/57, Boston Bruins; 1964/65 to 1966/67, Toronto Maple Leafs; 1967/68, Los Angeles Kings; 1969/70, New York Rangers

NHL

		Regular Season								Playoffs				
GP	W	L	T	MIN	GA	Sho.	GAA	GP	W	L	MIN	GA	Sho.	GAA
971	447	330	172	57194	2389	103	2.51	106	54	48	6290	266	12	2.54

NHL Feats: Hockey Hall of Fame (1971); RS Career Rank – second in shutouts (103), third in games in goal (971) and minutes played (57,194), and fifth in wins (447); Vezina Trophy (outstanding goaltender) in '52, '53, '55 & '65 (shared); Calder Memorial Trophy (outstanding rookie) in '51; Seven All-Star selections – First Team from '51 to '53 and Second Team in '54, '55, '59 & '63; #1 RS wins from '51 to '55, shutouts in '51, '52 & '55 and goals-against average in '52 & '53; Stanley Cup winning clubs (five) – Detroit in '50, '52, '54 & '55 and Toronto in '67; The Red Wings retired his #1.

AHL

		Regular Season								Playoffs				
GP	W	L	T	MIN	GA	Sho.	GAA	GP	W	L	MIN	GA	Sho.	GAA
128	69	37	12	7680	393	5	3.07	10	8	2	600	21	0	2.10

AHL Feats: Dudley "Red" Garrett Memorial Award (outstanding rookie) in 1948/49; First Team All-Star in 1949/50; Skated with Calder Cup winning Indianapolis in 1949/50.

Billy Smith
Goaltender

Two AHL seasons: 1970/71 & 1971/72, Springfield Kings
18 NHL seasons (1971/72 to 1988/89): 1971/72, Los Angeles Kings; 1972/73 to 1988/89, New York Islanders

NHL

	Regular Season								Playoffs					
GP	W	L	T	MIN	GA	Sho.	GAA	GP	W	L	MIN	GA	Sho.	GAA
680	305	233	105	38431	2031	22	3.17	132	88	36	7645	348	5	2.73

NHL Feats: Hockey Hall of Fame (1993); Vezina Trophy (outstanding goaltender) in 1981/82; William M. Jennings Trophy (lowest team RS GAA) in 1982/83 (shared); Conn Smythe Trophy (PY MVP) in 1982/83; First Team All-Star in 1981/82; #1 RS wins in 1981/82; Stanley Cup winning clubs (four) – New York Islanders from 1979/80 to 1982/83; The Islanders retired his #31.

AHL

	Regular Season								Playoffs					
GP	W	L	T	MIN	GA	Sho.	GAA	GP	W	L	MIN	GA	Sho.	GAA
77	32	30	11	4377	237	6	3.25	15	10	3	874	42	1	2.88

AHL Feats: #1 RS shutouts in 1971/72; Skated with Calder Cup winning Springfield in 1970/71.

Clint Smith
Center

Two AHL seasons (1936/37 & 1951/52): 1936/37, Philadelphia Ramblers; 1951/52, Cincinnati Mohawks

11 NHL seasons (1936/37 to 1946/47): 1936/37 to 1942/43, New York Rangers; 1943/44 to 1946/47, Chicago Black Hawks

NHL

	Regular Season					Playoffs			
GP	G	A	Pts.	PIM	GP	G	A	Pts.	PIM
483	161	236	397	24	42	10	14	24	2

NHL Feats: Hockey Hall of Fame (1991); Lady Byng Memorial Trophy (most gentlemanly player) in 1938/39 & 1943/44; #1 RS assists in 1943/44; Top 10 RS points in five seasons, assists in four seasons and goals in three seasons; Skated with the Stanley Cup winning New York Rangers in 1939/40.

AHL

	Regular Season					Playoffs			
GP	G	A	Pts.	PIM	GP	G	A	Pts.	PIM
51	25	29	51	17	6	4	3	7	0

AHL Feats: Top 10 RS points, goals and assists in one season.

210

Allan Stanley
Defense

Three AHL seasons: 1946/47 to 1948/49, Providence Reds
21 NHL seasons (1948/49 to 1968/69): 1948/49 to 1954/55, New York Rangers; 1954/55 & 1955/56, Chicago Black Hawks; 1956/57 & 1957/58, Boston Bruins; 1958/59 to 1967/68, Toronto Maple Leafs; 1968/69, Philadelphia Flyers

NHL

Regular Season					Playoffs				
GP	G	A	Pts.	PIM	GP	G	A	Pts.	PIM
1244	100	333	433	792	109	7	36	43	80

NHL Feats: Hockey Hall of Fame (1981); Stanley Cup winning clubs (four) – Toronto from 1961/62 to 1963/64 & 1966/67; Three All-Star selections – Second Team in 1959/60, 1960/61 & 1965/66.

AHL

Regular Season					Playoffs				
GP	G	A	Pts.	PIM	GP	G	A	Pts.	PIM
145	24	61	85	137	5	0	0	0	4

AHL Feats: Skated with Calder Cup winning Providence in 1948/49.

AHL INDIVIDUAL AWARD HISTORY

Name (seasons)	Description
Aldege "Baz" Bastien Memorial Award (1983/84 to the present)	Outstanding Goaltender (best at his position); Bastien had four great seasons in the AHL with the Pittsburgh Hornets before his pro career was cut short by an eye injury in training camp in Sept. of 1949; He served in many capacities with several AHL clubs after retiring as a player: Pittsburgh Hornets – business manager (1950/51 to 1952/53, 1961/62 & 1962/63), general manager (1963/64 to 1966/67) and head coach (1949/50, 1953/54, 1962/63 & 1966/67); Hershey Bears – business manager (1956/57 to 1960/61); and Baltimore Skipjacks – alternate governor (1982/83); The all-star netminder passed away during 1982/83.
Jack A. Butterfield Trophy (1983/84 to the present)	Playoff Most Valuable Player; Butterfield has the longest tenure of any Chairman of the Board on the AHL Board of Governors (16 seasons from 1994/95 to the present) and had the longest tenure of any AHL president (28 seasons from 1966/67 to 1993/94); He was league treasurer from 1972/73 to 1993/94; Butterfield was general manager of the Springfield Indians from 1957/58 to 1966/67 and was the club's head coach for part of 1965/66; Member of the Hockey Hall of Fame (class of 1980) and AHL Hall of Fame (2006).
Les Cunningham Award (1947/48 to the present)	Regular Season Most Valuable Player; Cunningham retired after 1946/47 as the AHL's all-time leader in RS points and assists and the AHL's all-time leader in PY points, goals, assists and games played; He is a member of the AHL Hall of Fame (2009).
Yanick Dupre Memorial Award (1997/98 to the present)	AHL Man of the Year; The player who best represents the spirit of Yanick Dupre with his involvement in the community; Dupre was a member of the Hershey Bears from 1992/93 to 1995/96 and lost his life to leukemia in August of 1997.
Thomas Ebright Award (1997/98 to the present)	Outstanding Contributions to the AHL; Ebright was the owner of the Baltimore Skipjacks and the Portland Pirates, and was a longtime member of the AHL Board of Governors until his death in 1997.
Jack Fox Memorial Award (1947/48 to 1950/51)	Outstanding player to combine sportsmanship with effective playing ability; Fox was a Canadian war hero, who was killed in the service of his country during World War II; He played with the Syracuse Stars in 1937/38 & 1938/39.
Dudley "Red" Garrett Memorial Award (1947/48 to the present)	Outstanding Rookie; Garrett gave his life during World War II while serving in the Canadian Navy; He was a member of the Providence Reds in 1942/43.
James C. Hendy Memorial Award (1961/62 to the present)	Outstanding Executive; The executive who has made the most outstanding contribution to the AHL; Hendy was the Cleveland Barons' general manager from 1949/50 to 1960/61; Also held the title of vice-president with the Barons; Hockey Hall of Fame inductee (1968).
Harry "Hap" Holmes Memorial Award (1947/48 to the present)	Lowest Goals-Against Average/Lowest Team Goals-Against Average; From 1947/48 to 1970/71, the award was presented to the goaltender with the lowest goals-against average who appeared in at least 50% of regular season games; Since 1971/72, the award has honored the goaltender or goaltenders on the team with the lowest goals-against average, providing each goaltender appeared in a minimum of 25 regular season games; Holmes, a Hall of Fame goaltender (1972), brought professional hockey to Cleveland in 1929/30 as owner of the Cleveland Indians (later known as the Falcons and the Barons); He was the owner/general manager/head coach of the Cleveland team until 1933/34; Holmes stayed on as the club's head coach through 1935/36 and general manager through 1936/37; He returned as head coach as a midseason replacement in 1936/37.

Name (seasons)	Description
Tim Horton Trophy (1978/79 to 1994/95)	Canadian-based Team Outstanding Player; The top two players (a winner and a runner-up) on the roster of a Canadian-based team who have accumulated the most points from the media Three Star Selections at all games during the regular season; Horton is one of the greatest defensemen of all-time and a Hockey Hall of Famer (1977); He skated with the Pittsburgh Hornets from 1949/50 to 1951/52.
Fred T. Hunt Memorial Award (1977/78 to the present)	Sportsmanship, Determination and Dedication to Hockey; Hunt was the general manager of the Buffalo Bisons from 1952/53 to 1969/70 and the Cincinnati Swords in 1972/73 & 1973/74; He also served on the AHL Board of Governors for both the Bisons and the Swords; Hunt played in eight AHL seasons (1940/41 ◇ 1948/49) with the Springfield Indians, the Buffalo Bisons and the Hershey Bears.
Wally Kilrea Award (1947/48)	Most Regular Season Points; The scoring leader award was originally named in Kilrea's honor because at the time he held the regular season record for most points in one season (99 points in 1942/43); Kilrea played seven seasons in the AHL from 1937/38 to 1943/44 with the Pittsburgh Hornets and the Hershey Bears.
Carl Liscombe Trophy (1948/49 to 1953/54)	Most Regular Season Points; The scoring leader award was renamed after Liscombe because he surpassed Wally Kilrea's mark for most points in one season (118 points in 1947/48); When the scoring leader award was first initiated in 1947/48, it was decided to re-name the trophy if any player set a new record, naming it after that player; Liscombe skated in eight AHL seasons (1936/37 ◇ 1949/50) with the Pittsburgh Hornets, the Indianapolis Capitols, the St. Louis Flyers and the Providence Reds.
Willie Marshall Award (2003/04 to the present)	Most Regular Season Goals; Marshall has held the AHL's all-time record for regular season points, goals and assists since the early 1970; He once held or shared the playoff all-time record for points, goals and assists for many years; He is a member of the AHL Hall of Fame (2006).
Ken McKenzie Award (1977/78 to the present)	Outstanding Executive – Public Relations and Marketing; Individual who accomplished the most during the season in promoting his or her AHL team; McKenzie was the co-founder and longtime president and publisher of *The Hockey News*.
Louis A. R. Pieri Memorial Award (1967/68 to the present)	Outstanding Coach; Pieri was the owner/president of the Providence Reds from 1939/40 up until he passed away in the summer of 1967; He also was the Reds' general manager/manager for many seasons; Pieri is a member of the AHL Hall of Fame (2009).
Eddie Shore Award (1958/59 to the present)	Outstanding Defenseman; Owner of the Springfield Indians/Kings ('40 to '42, '47 to '51 & '55 to '76) and the Syracuse Warriors ('52 to '54); He was general manager/manager of the Indians ('40 to '57), the Buffalo Bisons ('43 to '45), the New Haven Eagles ('46) and the Warriors ('52 to '54) and was head coach of the Indians in '55; Hockey Hall of Fame inductee ('47) and AHL Hall of Fame inductee ('06).
John B. Sollenberger Trophy (1954/55 to the present)	Most Regular Season Points; When George Sullivan of the Hershey Bears (119 points in 1953/54) surpassed Carl Liscombe's mark for points in one season the league decided to give the scoring leader trophy a permanent name instead of changing it in the future, whenever any player sets a new regular season one season points record; Sollenberger was AHL president in 1953/54 and the Chairman of the AHL Board of Governors from 1957/58 to 1965/66 (Honorary Chairman in 1966/67); He was also the Hershey Bears' president from 1938/39 to 1961/62 and the club's general manager/manager from 1938/39 to 1949/50.

214

RESOURCES

Publications/Information Credits

American Hockey League
American Hockey League Media Guide, Official Guide and Record Book, Press-TV-Radio Guide, and Red Book, 1945/46 to 2010/11
American Hockey League team programs (various teams and seasons)
Atchue, A.J. – Coordinator Communications, American Hockey League
Bacon, Whit (SIHR member)
Before the Blade by Tim Warchocki
Bitoue, Miragh, Hockey Hall of Fame
Fitzsimmons, Ernie (SIHR member)
Forgotten Glory – The Story of the Cleveland Barons by Gene Kiczek
Goodman, Bob (SIHR member)
High Sticks and Hat Tricks – A History of Hockey in Cleveland by Gene Kiczek
Hockey Hall of Fame, Toronto, Canada
Hockey In Providence by Jim Mancuso
Hockey In Springfield by Jim Mancuso
Hockey In Syracuse by Jim Mancuso
National Hockey League Official Guide & Record Book, 2011
O'Hanley, Don (SIHR member)
Slate's, Ralph (SIHR member) Hockey Data Base (hockeydb.com)
Society for International Hockey Research (SIHR) website (www.sihrhockey.org)
The Hockey News (various issues and years)
The Sporting News Hockey Guide and Register (various years)
Total Hockey (Second Edition) – The Official Encyclopedia of the National Hockey League

Photo Credits

American Hockey League
Bacon, Whit (SIHR member)
Binghamton Senators (AHL)
Campbell, Craig (SIHR member), HHOF Manager Images/Archival Services
Fitzsimmons, Ernie (SIHR member)
Gladu, Roger
Hockey Hall of Fame, Toronto, Canada
Kiczek, Gene
Krenzer, Kristen, Director of Media Relations, Binghamton Senators
Leger, Ron (SIHR member)
Society for International Hockey Research (SIHR) website (www.sihrhockey.org)

JIM MANCUSO
AUTHOR

Jim Mancuso is a minor league hockey historian and aficionado who has written many books and numerous articles on minor league hockey teams and leagues. His main goals are to preserve and promote the minor league hockey history of North America through publications and by maintaining an accurate archive of minor league hockey players, teams and leagues. Jim's books include <u>20 Years of the ECHL</u>, <u>The Clinton Comets: An EHL Dynasty</u>, <u>The Clinton Comets: From The Chenango Canal to National Champions</u>, <u>Hockey In the Capital District</u> (New York), <u>Hockey In Charlotte</u>, <u>Hockey In Portland</u> (Oregon), <u>Hockey In Providence</u>, <u>Hockey In Springfield</u>, <u>Hockey In Syracuse</u> and <u>Hockey Night In Utica – Featuring the Comets, the Mohawks and the Stars</u>. He also wrote and compiled the Southern Professional Hockey League's (SPHL) inaugural media guide for the circuit's 5th Anniversary season in 2008/09.

He earned a B.A. "cum laude" in Sociology from St. John Fisher College and an M.A. in Applied Social Research from West Virginia University. Jim works and teaches in the field of Sociology. He is a vice-president (USA East) of the Society for International Hockey Research (SIHR), is a member of the Rhode Island Reds Heritage Society, belongs to the Springfield Hockey Heritage Society and is a member of the Pi Gamma Mu International Social Science Honorary (inducted in 1989). Jim was born in Utica, New York, where he currently resides. His daughter Miriam (nine) loves to watch hockey games and go skating with her dad.

Ernie Fitzsimnmons
Photo Editor

Ernie is a Hockey Historian from Fredericton, New Brunswick who has authored his own book on the early history of Fredericton Hockey (up to 1945), as well as co-authoring Total Hockey 1 and 2 and From Pond To Pro, a history of hockey in Moncton, New Brunswick. He is working on a second book on Fredericton's history that will bring it up to 1979.

His two main areas of expertise are in recreating statistics of long lost Pro and amateur leagues, by painstaking research on Microfilm readers of old newspapers that result in a set of modern type statistics and in gathering over 50,000 different hockey photos. He only counts having one photo of Gordie Howe in Detroit, even though he has countless photos of the great and all other players who stayed with one team for many years, so the number is likely at least three times 50,000. He also donated over 20,000 photos to the Hockey Hall of Fame along with hockey card sets.

He was invited by *The Hockey News* as a selector to help pick the top 50 players of all-time and recently to bring the top 100 players list up to date.

Ernie was one of the Society For International Hockey Research (SIHR) founding 17 members that were invited to Kingston, Ontario in 1991 by Bill Fitsell. Since that time he has served 4 years as Executive VP, 4 more as the President and one as the Secretary of SIHR.

Since the SIHR database was added to the website in 2003 he has been a prime mover in adding information and scanning (over 30,000) photos to the site. He also copied many years of final league stats and sent to other members to help input on the site.

Because of his accumulation of information over the past 40 years, Ernie is regularly consulted by *The Hockey News*, Hockey Hall of Fame, Media members and individuals trying to recreate information on their family members.

His working career was as an Air Traffic Controller with the Canadian Government, but he also dabbled in hockey on the side as Sports Editor of the Gander Beacon in Newfoundland and as Statistician for both the AHL Fredericton Express and Canadiens in the 1980's and 90's.

He has written many articles for Newspapers and Magazines over the years, including the Fifty Year History of the AHL and the IHL History and was a regular contributor of photos to the AHL Guide.

Ernie's wife Marlene is also a SIHR member, while his daughter Tina (Ottawa fan) and son Rob (Montreal) are both avid hockey fans.